PROTECTIVE ORDER

The Disarming of America and

Destruction of the American Way of Life

A. ROGER CHARLES

Protective Order

The Disarming of America and

Destruction of the American Way of Life

By A. Roger Charles

ISBN-13: 978-1522883104
ISBN-10: 152288310X

Published by Mifflin Brown & Co.

Prologue

"PROTECTIVE ORDER, The Disarming of America and the Destruction of the American Way of Life," is inspired by a set of true facts. Although many names and locations have been slightly altered, the facts involved arising out of actions of the North Castle Police Department and Courthouse in Armonk, New York are set forth without alteration and described with specificity.

As the reader will learn, the protagonist, Thomas Strahan, is a distinguished American over seventy years of age. He has impeccable credentials as a law-abiding citizen with a long history of service to others, both nationally and internationally. As such, he has received many awards and much recognition during the course of a distinguished life. He believes in the "Right to Bear Arms" as set forth in the 2nd Amendment, but has sometimes in the past disagreed with the NRA when he believed positions taken by it were not defensible (e.g., opposition to certain measures to restrict the sale of guns to felons and to those with severe mental problems).

However, after living through the facts of this case and reflecting on the very personal conversations he once had with one of his law clients, Charlton Heston, he has come to appreciate the "camel's nose under the tent" concerns that were posited by Heston. As Strahan learns the hard way, it is not the enemy without, but rather the enemy within – that is, the government itself, that Americans must most vigilantly guard against.

As the facts of this narrative evolve, the reader will learn that Mr. Strahan was rather obviously framed by one who has over the course of her life committed numerous crimes, including felonies, for which she has never been prosecuted due among other reasons to the expiration of the Statute of Limitations. She is also known to be a pathological liar caused, in part, by serious mental instabilities. It is by choice that she is here known as Satha Naar, as Satha in Hindi is often given to one who is dishonest.

In short, the facts set forth in this book are so bizarre and surreal that they would be difficult to make up – yet again they are absolutely true. It is a story of massive and continuous government malfeasance, misfeasance, bias, ineptitude, and negligence, and evidences the extent to which our most basic and fundamental liberties are being eroded, almost on a daily basis. It also evidences that no one, no matter how honorable, is immune from tyrannical institutions or individuals when they act under color of authority.

Finally, this story demonstrates just how easy it would be for a court (even the smallest and, arguably, one of the least significant in size and importance in the entire United States) to completely disarm the citizenry and to dispossess people not just of their guns, but also of their homes and personal effects, even when they did not commit and are not convicted of any criminal conduct whatever.

But it is not just the judicial system that has run amok. This book goes further as it warns against government overreach by demonstrating that it's not just in cities like Baltimore, New York, and Ferguson that many law enforcement authorities have assumed the mind-set of military style forces whose authority cannot be questioned. It can happen even in a community as bucolic as Bedford, NY. Yes, this is a story about absolute tyranny by governmental institutions run amok and, if it can occur in Bedford, most assuredly it can occur anywhere in our land.

Constitutional rights and liberties are sacred, but they are being eroded in our country one by one. Hopefully this story, inspired by actual facts, will help awaken people to the severity of the situation for the time for action is NOW – before it is too late.

Table of Contents

Chapter 1

It was a rather cold fall afternoon in the quaint, but historic, small village of Bedford, New York. Winter was fast approaching and frost would soon be on the way. Thomas Strahan was working out in the basement of his large three-story home under the guidance of his friend and personal trainer, Larry Sawyer. It would never have occurred to him that on that day, or on any day for that matter, officers from the North Castle Police Department would arrive at this home to evict and arrest him.

After all, Tom was a seventy-year-old retired attorney, former law professor, and former Judge who had received much recognition over the course of a rather distinguished career. In fact, Thomas Strahan was not only a law abiding man, but was sufficiently renown for his worldwide humanitarian work and adventurous spirit that he had once dined as the Queen's guest at Buckingham Palace, led an expedition rafting the dangerous whitewater rapids of the Urubamba River in South America, escaped with only minor wounds from an attack by a mountain lion while backpacking alone in the Sierra Nevada Mountains, and had often engaged in his humanitarian efforts in areas of the lesser developed world where malaria, dengue fever and other deadly diseases were rampant.. Yet, from a medical standpoint, he should not even have been able to lift a spoon to his mouth; run a comb through his slightly wavy hair or, frankly, even use a piece of toilet paper to wipe his bottom.

In 2002, nearly ten years prior to the moment of the police officers' unexpected arrival, Tom had been lying in a hospital bed with an oxygen line in his nose, a tracheal tube down his throat, an IV needle in his wrist, and a catheter in his urethra. He also had a variety of wired sensors monitoring his breathing, his heartbeat, and his brain function, all thanks to being struck by an off-duty delivery truck driver registering a blood alcohol content of 0.29. Needless to say, the prospects for Tom at that time were, to put it mildly, extremely grim. In fact, Tom had already flatlined three times, and the doctors could not understand how his heart had resumed beating after stopping several times. How Tom had gone on to again talk, walk, sing, mountain bike, ski, play tennis, and make love—even to have survived at all—was a mystery to most medical professionals. Doctors would regularly scratch their heads when Tom told them what he had been through: leg fractures in multiple places, paralysis from the neck down, and clinical death. Most medical professionals could not believe he had gone on to live not in a vegetative or paralytic state but as a high-functioning human being and philanthropist who now traveled internationally to help end hunger, promote literacy, and improve health conditions in remote villages throughout the developing world.

In the first days after Tom had awakened from the surgeries that had saved his life, he was told by his doctor—Dr. Monahan, a caring and thoughtful but realistic man—that he'd likely never walk again. "Screw that," Tom thought as the doctor delivered this apparent life sentence. "I'll be walking again before the year is through."

Tom, who had grown up in the 1940s in rural Kentucky in a home with no running water or electricity and who had been picking cotton in the fields of Texas by the age of eleven years, had always been a bit of a rebellious cuss. It had been his determination and mental fortitude—some might even have called it obstinacy—that had allowed him to live on his own since he was fifteen years old. Tom had put himself through seven years of college and law school while working two to three jobs at a time so he'd have enough money to pay for food, rent, car, gas money, tuition, and, eventually, a wife and an unexpected baby.

It was that very determination and stubbornness that Tom used to teach himself how to walk again on his own while recovering at home. And he did this when his physicians insisted that he not take the risk to even try for fear that he would end up back in the hospital, and possibly dead. But Tom felt that he could not listen to the doctors. It was his body and his mind after all and, quite frankly, he feared he might go insane if he did not at least try to walk again.

Moreover, learning to walk again hadn't been his only struggle during that troubled time. He'd also experienced the loss of his older brother to a rare and painful form of cancer just seven months earlier. He'd lost his mother shortly after his brother to what the doctors deemed a broken heart. And he'd lost his wife of over thirty-five years to separation and divorce. So Tom was willing to die trying to walk again, because accepting life's blows without pushing back would to him be a sort of death anyway.

And so, on one rather gray California afternoon, as the wind and rain howled outside his window and as he heard his wife's car drive away, Tom decided that this was his moment. He reached out to his marble-topped bedside table with his left hand and pushed down in an effort to prop himself up in bed, but he experienced no movement.

He fell back in exhaustion. With his muscles severely atrophied by a three-month lack of use, he sensed that it was too much for his traumatized body to push up from that position. Tom rested for a brief moment where he lay on the left side of the bed and then gathered his thoughts.

He decided he would try a different tack. Maybe if he could get closer to the edge of his bed, that would help him swing at least one leg over the edge. He used what little strength he could muster in his upper body and began pulling and scooting himself ever so slowly to the left, inch by inch, centimeter by centimeter. Bit by bit, he dragged his body until he had successfully aligned himself with the edge of the bed. Below was the solidity of the floor. As he imagined what it might feel like to touch the surface of the floor again with his feet, Tom's stomach did a little cartwheel.

And then he went for it.

He grabbed his left leg with his left arm, which still had a slight bit of feeling in it, and dragged it over the edge and toward the floor. Then, with that same hand, he reached across his body and succeeded in pulling his right leg over the edge as well: a small miracle, really! It was a clumsy, unrefined movement that sent Tom's whole frame sliding off of the bed, with his head nearly hitting the marble top of his bedside table on the way down.

Less determined human beings might have started sobbing, cursed God in anger, or railed with frustration, terror, or rage, but not Thomas Strahan. He lay there on his bedroom floor, soothed by the feel of its soft shag carpet beneath his back. He stared up at his ceiling and smiled. It was a shit-eating sort of grin that said, "I told you so." He felt the same sense of triumph that he had felt years ago in high school when he had stolen the competing high school's stone eagle mascot during the night and placed it on the front steps of his own school. The fact was that he had gotten out of bed on his own for the first time in three months and that fall, to Thomas Strahan, had been the first step on his journey to walking again.

* * *

Before the passing of the 365th day after that fall, Tom had indeed taught himself to walk again. It had been an ugly affair with much dragging and bruising, prodding and falling. But he had done it, pretty much on his own at home, with only limited help by his physical therapists and none from his soon-to-be ex-wife (who was claiming to friends that she was nursing him back to health). In a relatively short period of time, Tom had made it down the stairs to the first floor of his home without falling or breaking his neck (which could easily have happened given the way he'd had to balance on the banister and use his left hand to drag his right leg down to the next step and then use that same left hand to move his left leg). It had taken some time before his walk had returned somewhat to normal, but bit by bit with practice at home and eventually out of the home intensive physical therapy, Tom gained back many of his former physical faculties and reached the level of health that he needed to attack life again with his characteristic passion and gusto.

Little did he realize when he encountered officers of the North Castle, New York, Police Department almost ten years later that he would be opening the door to a legal struggle that would be just as arduous and harrowing as learning to walk again and that would require the same level of herculean effort to overcome.

Chapter 2

The truth was that Thomas Strahan's life had always been lived at the extremes, so surviving near-death experiences and escaping the clutches of paralysis almost made sense. His life had been full of highs and lows, which meant that over the years he had enjoyed the company of many interesting people and traveled to some amazing parts of the world. He had also earned himself a substantial livelihood serving as legal counsel for some of the world's best known celebrities and largest corporations while, at the same time, offering free legal representation to individuals and organizations along the way to advocate for causes in which he believed.

On the flip side, Tom had never had things easy. He had grown up in a small farming community and in a home without electricity or plumbing, so trips to the outhouse in the cold of winter were the norm; he had watched his father fail at business while treating Tom's mother quite poorly. And Tom had lived on his own since he was fifteen years old, attending school in the daytime while working jobs in the early mornings, evenings, and nights to cover all of the costs of living. If Tom was going to eat at night, it would be with the quarters and dollars he had made mowing lawns, doing stoop field labor, and putting together widgets in the local factory. Yes, the highs had been high and the lows had been low, and that just seemed to be the way of things for Tom.

Perhaps, then, it should not have been such a surprise that his business venture with Satha Naar, once full of hope and possibility, would end with two police officers in his kitchen, telling him they were there to evict him from his own home.

When Tom had met Satha Naar in 2002, she had presented herself to him as a Professor of Epidemiology at Columbia University; author of a book addressing ways to prevent major and life threatening diseases; and protégé of the famed Dr. Mehmet Oz, the cardiothoracic surgeon, advocate of complementary medicine and host of the popular *Dr. Oz Show*. Until recently, Tom and Satha had been partners in a nutritional supplements business known as Quintessence of Life.

Although Satha had recently moved out, she, along with Tom, co-owned as Tenant's in Common the house in which they lived. Tom's household also included his daughter, Ashley, twenty-two years old, who had left an unhappy college stint out west to come and live with her father on the east coast. Tom also had his faithful dog, Hercules, with him.

After living in the same large house with Satha and interacting with her every day, Tom had come to realize that the image Satha had presented to Tom had cracks beneath the surface, cracks that would soon widen into chasms. Unfortunately, Tom had only recently discovered those cracks at great personal cost, financial and otherwise. And one of the ways he was paying had brought officers from the North Castle Police Department to his home.

The announcement of the officers' arrival had actually come down the stairs from Tom's daughter, Ashley, a little after five o'clock in the afternoon. "Dad! There are some police officers here to see you," she called. She was baffled and yet not overly worried, as she knew no man with more integrity than her own father. Perhaps they were there to let her dad know about some criminal activity in the neighborhood? Maybe the officers wanted to inform them of some recent break-ins at one of their neighbors' homes. After all, the house was located in the high-net-worth bedroom community of Bedford, not far north of New York City. These thoughts however weren't very likely, as Bedford was nestled in bucolic Westchester County, which had one of the lowest rates of crime in the state of New York.

As Tom climbed the basement stairs to see what was going on, he caught a glimpse of a tall and sturdy uniformed police officer standing at the top of the stairs in the doorway behind his blonde-haired, blue-eyed daughter, whose tiny frame did little to eclipse the man. Even as Tom ascended, he could still hear the clinks and clangs of his fitness trainer in the basement gym rearranging some weights and putting them back in their proper spots. Although it was nearly time for their appointment to end, Tom was unperturbed that he had been called off the treadmill in the last ten minutes of his run. Having traveled to parts of the world where it was a challenge to get a clean glass of water to drink or enough food to fill one's belly—and having grown up in rustic conditions himself—Tom had the kind of life perspective that kept his temper on an even keel the majority of the time. Life was unpredictable, and nothing was guaranteed. However, he didn't understand how a trained police officer had entered his home and walked through several rooms to get to where he was now standing unless he had a properly served search warrant or had probable cause to believe that a crime was in progress that required urgent action. Obviously, neither was the case here. Nevertheless, he decided to not do anything that might be perceived as belligerent.

As Tom neared the top of the stairs, his daughter and the police officer backed up and allowed Tom to pass into the kitchen with them. It was then that Tom saw the other uniformed officer, a man of middling height and stockier build than the first officer. This second officer was standing off to the side near the kitchen island. Both officers had an alertness about them that kept them holding their bodies stiffly with their arms by their sides, as if ready to reach to their waist belts and draw their firearms if necessary.

"Hello, officers," Tom said cordially, trying not to betray his confusion at their presence. "What brings you here today?"

The lead policeman—a Sergeant, it turned out— got straight to the point. He explained that they were there with a court order to evict Tom from his home.

Amazed, Tom stuttered, "For what reason?"

"We have an ex parte order of protection, obtained by a woman named Dr. Satha Naar, who states that you may have unregistered guns in the house," the Sergeant stated.

Tom blinked as he tried to register the officer's words. Order of protection? Protect Satha against what? She didn't even live here anymore. What's more, Tom didn't keep guns in the house. Yes, he had been gifted some guns by west coast law enforcement authorities in the 1960s and 1970s, some as a gesture of thanks, others to protect himself from death threats after he had put a dangerous gang leader behind bars.

But Tom hadn't even seen those guns in over ten years.

"I will, but let me say officers, I don't have any guns in this house—at least not to my knowledge. I want to see the Order to which you are referring. I also want to know by what authority you have entered my home without being invited."

The taller man who identified himself as Sergeant Huffman replied: "First of all, we don't have a copy of the Order with us, but it was issued by Judge Lysander of the North Castle Court. Second, this young lady didn't stop us when she opened the door so we went ahead and entered."

"So if a young 5'2" girl opens the door of a home and sees two uniformed and armed officers, both well over 6' tall towering over her, you think you have the right to just barge past her. Have you read the United States Constitution, officer?"

"Well, she didn't stop us and we're here. If you don't like it, you can take it up with the Judge," the Sergeant replied.

Tom knew that this wasn't the time to argue the Constitution with seemingly poorly trained officers so, rather than further irritate them, he scanned his mind to recall if there was any reason at all that there could be truth to what Sergeant Huffman was saying about weapons being inside the house.

Tom clarified, "Officers, I do own guns, but insofar as I know, they're either in the attic of my former home in Westwood, California, or they are stored in the garage of a friend of mine in Encino, California."

"Are you positive?" Sergeant Huffman questioned.

"Well, I certainly know they aren't in this house," Tom replied as he continued scanning his mind for clues to the truth. "But my friend, John Grant, who has been storing lots of my items in his home or in his garage, had some of the my things shipped here to me in my camper several months back. It's parked on this property, and the boxes inside the camper have never been opened since the camper arrived. But I can't believe that John would have sent guns back here to New York without telling me, at least not if he knew that guns were there."

Tom raised the small white gym towel from around his neck to wipe some beads of perspiration from his forehead and then continued. "It's highly unlikely, but I suppose it's possible that my guns are in one of the unsealed boxes in the camper. Anything is possible, I guess."

"Can we take a look?" Sergeant Huffman inquired, apparently wondering whether Mr. Strahan had something to hide.

It was a pivotal moment, a time when Tom could easily have said no to the officers since they did not have a search warrant. He knew as an attorney and from the decades that he had taught constitutional law what his Fourth Amendment right was. He could recite it to the letter in fact, as he had taught a whole class around it for years:

> The right of the people to be secure in their persons, houses, papers, and effects, against unreasonable searches and seizures, shall not be violated, and no Warrants shall issue, but upon probable cause, supported by Oath or affirmation, and particularly describing the place to be searched, and the persons or things to be seized.

Heck, didn't most Americans know the essence of the Fourth Amendment? All you had to do was watch a crime show on television to know the police had no right to search a person's home without a court order that was based on reasonable and probable cause.

As a result, Tom was not obligated by law to say yes to the officer's request to search his house. Yet he knew that he had nothing to hide. What's more, his inclination was to cooperate with the officers even though they obviously had unlawfully entered the premises. Anyway, Tom loved his country and felt that he should oblige the officers who, however inappropriately, were just doing their jobs as apparently they thought they had a right to do. Tom could later speak with their Chief about what seemed to be a lack of Constitutional knowledge. If anger was to be felt in this moment, it was toward Satha, who had managed to introduce pain into Tom's life once again.

"I suppose you already know exactly where the guns are if this lady filed a complaint about them," Tom responded.

'"Well," Sergeant Huffman replied, "strangely, Dr. Naar said that she has never been threatened and has never seen firearms in the home, but she thinks that they might be here somewhere. Where, she apparently has no idea."

Tom's stomach started to boil with anger. Although the officers themselves were clueless on the subject, Tom knew that Satha's claims about the firearms were no more than a scheme to get back at him for ending their business partnership, and for filing suit against her for money she owed him. Still, he again reminded himself that the two police officers in his kitchen were likely just there doing their jobs as they apparently felt they had a right to do. Why not let them search the house and discover for themselves that Satha's claim was ridiculous? Then this whole awkward business would be over and, he hoped, he and Ashley could salvage the rest of the night.

So Tom voluntarily granted the two officers permission to search the house for the guns in question. "Take your time, gentlemen," he said politely. "You have my permission to search, although I'll be more than shocked if you find anything." Then he asked Ashley to show the lower ranking officer, Officer Scherf, how to access the attic since its opening was fairly hidden.

"There's a light up in the attic," Tom explained, "and it's well lit so you can also comfortably examine the contents of any boxes you find there as well. Insofar as the camper is concerned, which is the only other place I could imagine that my guns could even possibly be, I don't have access to it right now because all of the various keys to the camper were taken by someone who used to live here. She's the same person you earlier mentioned by the title of *doctor.* However, she's no doctor and, as I said, when she moved out she took my keys with her and I haven't been able to access the camper since that time. In fact, I've never removed the boxes from the camper. But if you want to break into it, you have my permission to do so."

With that, Officer Scherf followed Ashley out of the kitchen, and Tom heard their footsteps going up the stairs.

"What's next?" Tom inquired of the other officer.

"I'll have to wait with you while my partner searches the house for guns," Sergeant Huffman explained.

Seeing that they would have some time to pass together, Tom invited the Sergeant into his office. They sat, each on one side of Tom's large antique cherry desk, as if at a scheduled meeting between lawyer and client, except now it was Tom who seemed to require legal representation. In fact, Tom explained to the officer that he'd like to reach out to counsel while they waited and opened his phone book to the number of the attorney he had retained to file a lawsuit against Satha a few weeks back. Satha had failed to pay Tom the $300,000 she had agreed to pay him to buy out his interest in their jointly owned business.

Tom held the ebony phone to his ear: It was the sturdy, old-fashioned kind that you lifted off of a four-sided trapezoidal base and held to your ear using one round end to listen and the other round end to speak. Tom had cordless phones in other parts of the house and, of course, a mobile phone but for his office he liked the quality and reliability of a standard telephone.

As Sergeant Huffman quietly examined the photos on Tom's desk—one of Tom sitting high on a camel's back with the Great Pyramids as a dusty backdrop; a photo of Tom's three children and several grandchildren standing in front of a green park bench with big smiles and bright eyes; and Tom's favorite, one of him in India with a gauzy array of colorful, hand-woven scarves around his neck and a group of villagers standing behind him offering welcome—Tom listened to the ring of the telephone droning on and off, on and off, on and off. Finally, a professional recording came on explaining that the law offices were closed and would not reopen until the following morning.

Suddenly, a wave of irritation washed over Tom. Why had the police chosen to arrive at the close of business anyway? Was it inconsiderate, clumsy, or perhaps intentional? If you assumed a person was guilty of keeping unregistered guns in his house or, perhaps worse, was the kind of character who might wrongfully use guns against another human being, maybe you owed them no courtesy at all.

Tom hung up the phone and did his best to shake off the sudden feeling that he was quite alone in the world. He decided to make the best of his time sitting there by speaking with the officer.

"I do own firearms, Sergeant, although to the best of my knowledge they are still in storage back west, where each one is properly licensed and registered," Tom began.

"Yes, you mentioned that earlier," Sergeant Huffman replied, unswayed from his staid demeanor.

"And though I own guns, I have never purchased a single one. They were all given to me," Tom continued. "In fact, I've never purchased a gun in my life."

Sergeant Huffman said nothing but appeared to listen a little more closely, as if trying to determine which side of the law Tom was on.

Tom proceeded to tell Sergeant Huffman the story of each of the guns he owned. One was a Smith & Wesson 9 mm given to him brand new by the Los Angeles County Sheriff for purposes of self-protection in 1967. Tom had received a death threat from a violent and notorious gang in the Los Angeles area after he had prosecuted and won a jury conviction

24

against the gang leader. The same death threats had been made against the county's District Attorney as well as the Governor of California, at the time Ronald Reagan. At the same time, Tom was also given a concealed weapon permit, which was and is incredibly hard to obtain in California. However, due to Tom being a responsible citizen with no criminal record or background of violence, his position as a prosecutor, and given the recent death threats, the authorities felt that Tom should be granted a permit so he could protect himself if the need to do so should occur.

Upon the occasion of his retirement from public service, Tom continued, the former Police Chief of Los Angeles and later State Senator representing Los Angeles County and a former candidate for Governor of the state had given him a complete set of LAPD official weaponry with holster, belt, and gun. Tom thought of those as collector's items and he had never even tried on the belt, much less fired the gun. He had also received the gift of a shotgun from the local sheriff's association, also upon the occasion of his retirement.

"Oh yes," Tom continued as he ran through the mental list of guns in his collection, "I also received a rifle in 1965 from my then father-in-law and I was given an antique and rusted pre–Spanish Civil War pistol from a friend upon his return from a trip to Europe. That gun is, as you can imagine, inoperable but it could have value to a collector."

Sergeant Huffman appeared to be intrigued by what he was learning of Tom's gun collection. Tom had made it clear that much of his collection had been given to him by law enforcement officials. He'd also persisted in maintaining his polite demeanor and tone in order to convey to Sergeant Huffman the respect he had for law enforcement officers. From what Tom could see, his approach seemed to be softening Sergeant Huffman.

In contrast, Tom found himself getting more and more worked up. He knew that his integrity was at stake here, and he found it hard to tolerate the idea that the Sergeant and his partner might believe that he had broken the law or was in any way an unsavory person.

"You know, Sergeant, even though I had a concealed weapon permit, I never, NOT ONCE in my life, carried a weapon—any weapon—on my person or even in my car, except when I went through training sessions as required by California law," explained Tom. "My law enforcement friends thought that I was crazy—that the death threats against me were legitimate and that I should take advantage of the permit. But you know, I just didn't want to carry a weapon. In fact, I went to the other extreme.

"With kids at home," Tom continued, and his tone softened as a vision entered his mind of his son and daughter during their childhoods padding around on the carpet in their pajamas, "I disassembled the guns and hid them where they couldn't possibly be found." Tom gave a small laugh and said, "Had I needed to use the guns in a hurry, I wouldn't have really been able to. But I felt more comfortable that way."

Although Sergeant Huffman did not break his professional demeanor and simply nodded, Tom suspected that the Sergeant was curious to hear more.

"You know, I've never discharged an automatic weapon in my life except during professional training," Tom continued. "I did go through training in ROTC during college, but only with rifles for purposes of marksmanship. And after I was given the Smith &

Wesson, I underwent training so I would know how to assemble and dissemble a handgun and the proper way to fire it. But beyond that, I never used any of my guns. In fact, the only time I really touched them after they were gifted to me was to bring two of them along whenever I renewed my concealed weapon permit every few years as required by California law.

"And you know, I haven't seen any of these guns since, to the best of my recollection, 1999. The last time I touched ANY of them was during my last recertification, when I got them out, put them together, and took them with me to the appropriate range that had been designated. Again that pertained only to two guns." Tom realized he might be repeating himself at this point, but he didn't care.

"And the last time I saw my guns, Sergeant Huffman, they were in the attic of my former home in Westwood, California."

Sergeant Huffman finally spoke. "Mr. Strahan, I really am sorry for the inconvenience today, but I hope you know that we are just doing our jobs. When the court issues an order, it's our job to execute it."

"Of course I realize that," Tom replied. "I just want to be clear to you that I am a law-abiding citizen with a long record of public service and that although I own guns which, to my knowledge are out West, I have only fired a couple of them for training purposes and some not at all.'"

Before Sergeant Huffman could respond and close to an hour having elapsed, Officer Scherf appeared in the doorway of the office looking a bit red-faced, as if he had been concentrating hard on something. "Well, there certainly aren't any guns in this house" he said, having finished his search in the attic as well as the rest of the house. He made eye contact with the Sergeant, who replied, "Well, I don't quite know what to do. We still have to evict you; we have a court order to do so. So you're going to have to leave right now."

"What?" Tom replied baffled. "My own home?"

"Well, yes. That's the court order," Sergeant Huffman explained.

Tom inhaled audibly and asked, "Well where . . . where will I stay?"

"Well, that's up to you," said Sergeant Huffman. "I mean, the first thing you have to do is come to the police station. We're not going to handcuff you, but you do have to go through what we always have people go through on these occasions."

Tom tried to push through the blinding shock he was now feeling. "And, uh, well, what about my daughter? What about my dog?"

"Well, the order doesn't pertain to them, so they can remain here at your home," the Sergeant said without the slightest hint of irony in his voice.

Until now, Tom had not let on that this whole situation was extremely awkward and discomfiting. But now he felt his grip on politeness slipping as he tried to understand why he was being asked to leave his home when he had done nothing wrong.

Each time he posed the question, the Sergeant would simply refer to the alleged, but never shown, court order. "I'm sorry, Mr. Strahan, but the order directs me to remove you from your home in order to protect one Dr. Satha Naar, who claims that you might have unregistered weapons in the house."

There might also be rocket-propelled grenades or ingredients to make chemical weapons stockpiled in a secret compartment beneath the basement, and Tom wondered what the court might have done if Satha had made such an accusation against him. Would a Judge, without hearing evidence and serving as both Judge and jury, simply issue a court order to have him executed due to treason?

And so it was that Tom found himself standing outside his own home in the dark at seven o'clock on a chilly October evening, wearing sweat-dried workout clothes and holding only a toothbrush, the sole item he had been allowed to take from his home before leaving, accompanied by the Sergeant and the other officer. He waved goodbye to Ashley, who was standing at the open door of the house, looking bewildered with her wide eyes and unbrushed hair, and told her that he was just going down to the police station to get everything straightened out. He'd be back tonight if he could, but he would most definitely return tomorrow.

Chapter 3

A prickly sensation ran down Tom's spine as he got into his car. He had forgotten to throw on a coat, but the chill that descended upon him was more than that. It was as if in stepping into the driver's seat and sitting down, he was displacing a lingering malevolence that was slow to disperse.

As Tom started his car ignition and adjusted his rearview mirror, he saw the lights of the police car behind him also go on. The officers clearly had faith that Tom, who had been cooperative throughout their visit and search, would meet them at a police station in Armonk, New York. The top of Ashley's head came into view in the mirror, and although Tom could not see Hercules, he imagined how Ashley's hand was still holding tight to Hercules's collar, her father's faithful dog standing beside her.

It was true that at the age of twenty-two years, Ashley was an adult, but in physical appearance her twenty-two was like some peoples sixteen. She was petite, did not yet have her driver's license, and she still depended on her father for many things. He drove her to her part-time job each day and paid for her food, housing, and clothes and for anything else she might need. Tom did not like the thought of leaving her alone in the house for the night and hoped that indeed he could get things resolved at the station this evening.

Tom detected some movement ahead of him and noticed that the police car had pulled ahead of him and was now heading down the long driveway with those absurd lights flashing, making Tom glad that his nearest neighbor was a few forested acres away. He stuck his hand outside his rolled-down window to wave one last goodbye to Ashley but pulled it in quickly as a blast of cold air swept through the car. As he began to pick up speed down the driveway, he closed the car window and settled for seeing the image of his daughter and their house grow more and more distant in the rear view mirror until it disappeared altogether and he had to refocus his eyes on the road before him.

Before turning right onto the country road to follow the police officers, Tom inhaled deeply, preparing for whatever lay ahead. He had climbed Mount Everest. He had put criminals in prison. He had held a dying Congolese child infected with dysentery in his arms. But nothing in his life had prepared him for this very strange moment when two police officers had arrived at his house and taken him into custody. He was a law-abiding citizen who paid his taxes, followed the speed limit, and picked up litter. He had never committed a crime of any type and, in fact, tried to give back as a leader in his community. He had raised a family, mentored inner-city youth, and offered a hand to many strangers on the street if he saw they needed his help. He had been in public service for more than fifteen years and was currently engaged in international humanitarian efforts in some of the poorest countries in the world. Tom was, to put it mildly, a model citizen, not someone who got arrested.

Yet now here he was being escorted to a police station. Nevertheless, things did appear to be going civilly enough. He was thankful the officers hadn't insisted on handcuffing him or putting him in the back of their squad car, but it was clear that if he had not followed the police officers' orders, he would have been forcibly detained. And why? Because someone had claimed that he might possess unregistered firearms in his home without, presumably, presenting a single shred of evidence. Based on what he had been told, he could only think, "what kind of Judge would issue an order of eviction without any cause whatever, much less probable cause?"

As Tom puzzled over the situation, he imagined that the trouble stemmed from the fact that he and Satha had formerly lived in the same large house and still currently co-owned the house from which he had just been removed. If a Judge had issued an eviction order against Tom, it must have stemmed from some claim by Satha that she wasn't safe at home with the supposedly unregistered guns, that she couldn't return home because of the guns, or that she was worried that Tom would try to use the guns against her. Surely, there must be something more than the officers knew or had been willing to share. The truth was that Satha and Tom had resided in the large, three-story home together as co-owners and business partners, not as lovers, for over four years without domestic disturbance. Satha had voluntarily decided to move out of the house a few weeks ago. Yes, there was a lawsuit between them that Tom has brought against Satha, as she had not followed through on her signed agreement to buy him out of his share of their business. But there was certainly no domestic discord between them as they did not have a domestic relationship, at least not in the common use of that phrase. This, however, the court would not know, given Satha's ability to weave lie after masterful lie. If the court had not pursued any due diligence before issuing the eviction order, how could a Judge know of Satha's incredible lifetime of lies, theft, and cheating?

"Christ, she had stolen nearly $1,500,000 from a bank in a mortgage fraud scam and then stashed the stolen money offshore in Singapore," Tom thought. She had been fraudulently calling herself a doctor who worked as a professor at Columbia University long after the university had contacted her and told her that she must cease and desist doing so. Her ex-husband had divorced her and none of her children would even speak to her. She had been seeing various psychiatrists for years, apparently for most of her life. She was not allowed to return to her home country of Singapore for reasons she never disclosed, and she had never paid U.S. taxes in the fifteen years or so she had lived in the United States. Over the years, little by little, Tom had learned that Satha's entire life was made up. It was simply a life of lies! But she presented herself as being quite spiritual, and person and after person, entity after entity, had believed her lies—the lies of a master con artist. Tom could feel the skin on his face growing warmer and warmer as he thought of it and of how dumb he had ben to believe her incredible lies until, one by one, they had come to light.

Of course, no matter how angry Satha's behavior made him feel, this was his problem now and he had to set about fixing it.

It took about twenty minutes for Thomas and the officers to reach the North Castle Police Station, which was oddly named because it was actually located in a small one-story building in the tiny hamlet of Armonk, New York. Tom recognized it immediately, having passed it many times on his way to the bank and the grocery store. He laughed as he recalled that North Castle itself could not even be found on a map. Instead, it was made up of the police station and the courthouse—both housed in the same building—and one ancillary building. These two buildings were located on a side street in Armonk, but the North Castle Police Department had jurisdiction not only over Armonk but also over the small village of Bedford. No one, not even the locals, could explain this structure, other than to say that it dated back to before the American Revolution. Perhaps some tinge of the colonial period still lingered in the building's corners, given the way operations were conducted here in a sort of monarchical fashion, which Tom unfortunately was soon to discover.

Tom parked and then followed the officers into the police station. He was directed to sit in a chair on the receiving side of a heavy metal desk that provided no view of its interior. The chair squeaked as Thomas sat down and faced Sergeant Huffman, who pulled up a screen on his computer. The litany of questions began: "Full name? Date of birth? Place of birth? Citizen of what country? Social security number? Place of residence?" and so on.

As Sergeant Huffman droned on and on, Tom answered each question honestly and diligently, although he did find himself getting slightly distracted by the number of police officers that were moving about the station. In fact, the number of officers milling about was somewhat of a surprise given how, as an avid newspaper reader—of local, national, and international publications—Tom was well aware that Westchester County had one of the lowest rates of crime in the state.

After Thomas's information had been entered into the police database, Sergeant Huffman said, almost apologetically, "Well, we have to take your photograph now."

"Fine, take a photograph," Tom said with resignation. Although he was irritated that he would have to get a mug shot taken, he was at least glad to see that Sergeant Huffman seemed to sense the ridiculousness of taking a mug shot of a seventy-year-old man who appeared unable to hurt a caterpillar, with not a single one of the alleged guns found in his home.

Nonetheless, Tom was sent into a room with another desk. This time, there was also a digital camera attached to a long, black, metal post that replaced the traditional tripod. Without looking up from her computer screen, the plainly dressed, heavyset woman behind the desk told Tom to stand on the marked spot on the floor and look straight into the lens. She did not have to touch the camera to adjust it but simply used her mouse and mouse pad to center the lens on Tom and zoom in. Tom felt like a huge mechanical eye was watching him, and he wondered who would have access to the photo once it was taken. The police station seemed small enough, but he knew how easily digital information could be circulated. He had nothing to hide, but the idea that he was now in the system from the criminal side of things really bothered him. It was one thing to be photographed by the media for bringing clean water to a poor village. But being captured on film for supposedly breaking the law inspired another feeling altogether. He could just imagine himself looking rough in the photograph by the mere fact of the lighting being so poor and his not having showered since that morning. Would gray circles under his eyes, salt-caked skin, and oily hair conspire to make him appear to be a guilty miscreant?

Tom emerged from the photo room and headed back toward Sergeant Huffman's desk, not knowing where else to go. Upon seeing Tom, Huffman stood up from his desk while swirling the coffee in the mug he held and said, "Time for fingerprinting," as he pointed to a window across the room.

Tom appeared to be the only detainee on the premises right then, and so he was first in line at the window. Another officer began to take his prints. Like Sergeant Huffman and all of the other officers milling around the station, he was very polite and thanked Tom for being so cooperative. Nonetheless, Tom couldn't shake the feeling that there was something slightly backward about this whole operation. The more time he spent in the police station, the more this feeling deepened.

When he had finally jumped through several of the necessary administrative hoops the police required, Tom was told that he would have to wait for the Judge to arrive to determine what would happen next in his case. He was told that she was actually a practicing attorney and ordinarily only appeared at the courthouse for an hour or so one evening every other week. So Tom sat at a bank of empty chairs, flipping through an old copy of a *National Geographic* magazine while trying to ignore the buzz of the vending machine. Officer Scherf offered him a coke, but Tom declined, as he made a habit of avoiding caffeine and added sugar.

An hour and a half passed, and it was now well into the evening hours when Thomas was finally told that the Judge had arrived and was ready to see him. Tom, who had been in courtrooms literally hundreds of times in his role as an attorney, was not overly nervous about heading into the courtroom. In fact, he was eager to have an opportunity to present his views and, he hoped, set things straight before a Judge. He followed another police officer into the courtroom which, it turned out, was but a box of a thing with gray linoleum floors, plain walls, and several rows of folding chairs. The Judge sat behind a bench, which was nothing more than a folding chair behind a long table. It was not on a raised platform, so Tom could see the Judge's feet in their plain shoes underneath the table. Only her nameplate, which read *Judge Eloise Lysander,* and the black robe that she wore over her clothes seemed to hint at some degree of professionalism, although they were hardly enough to offset the rest of the scenery.

"The Court of North Castle is now open on this twenty-third day of October at 8:42 in the evening," she said and hit her gavel on the wooden sound block, which resonated throughout the empty room. With her navy shoes shuffling under the table and the way that Judge Lysander seemed to hit the sound block harder than necessary, Tom found himself thinking that Judge Lysander seemed to be trying a bit too hard to appear Judge-like. Remembering how his Grandfather Strahan had always taught him to respect authority, however, Tom tried to shake this thought from his mind, stood silently before the Judge, and waited to hear what would come next.

"Mr. Strahan," Judge Lysander began, looking above her eyeglasses, which were worn low on the bridge of her nose, and not so much at Tom directly, "I ordinarily only convene court every other Tuesday evening at seven o'clock, so this is an unusual time and unusual day for me to be seeing a case. In fact, I find it quite an inconvenience to be here. As such, I'm not prepared to handle it at this time, so you will have to return to court tomorrow. In the meantime, I have issued a protective order restraining you from returning to your home tonight and you will have to find another place to stay until I can find a more convenient time to be here."

Tom found himself feeling so overwhelmed that he did not know what to say. Where to begin? He was struck by the fact that the court was only in session for one evening every other week. However, what was really weird to him—as an experienced attorney and law professor—was that the Judge was proceeding without even reading him his rights or telling him of any charges had been filed against him, a basic *arraignment,* as it's called at law. He was not told what the charges against him were, if any; he was not informed that he had right to counsel; and he was not asked to enter a plea to anything. Tom thought, "What kind of a podunk, rinky-dink operation is this?" Westchester County has the highest tax rate of any county in the United States, but this village courthouse was clearly not a priority insofar as capital outlay was concerned; nor should it have been. The only bright side of these proceedings was that the court agreed to release Tom from police custody without any bail requirements, as he was trusted to return the following day as requested. Tom, as he had done since shortly after five o'clock that evening upon first meeting the officers, cooperated and agreed to do so.

As the bailiff walked Tom out of the courtroom, he could hear Judge Lysander chatting rather loudly with a court attaché in irritated tones. He wasn't one hundred percent sure, but he thought he heard the Judge say something about a reality TV show that she would have to race home to watch and she didn't appreciate being called in, even if just briefly, on one of her irregular court evenings.

Tom, on the other hand, had no idea where home would be that night, and he turned his mind to figuring out where he could find a place to stay. Having spent most of his life in the west, he did not have many friends in the surrounding area and none with whom he could stay, especially on such short notice, not to mention that the whole ordeal of being removed from his home was rather embarrassing. Although the law itself required that all defendants be presumed innocent until proven guilty, he knew that people's psychology quite often worked in the opposite manner. After all, how could anyone in this position ever begin to explain such a bizarre occurrence as that through which he had just gone?

Chapter 4

It was dark and it was now late, and Tom found himself staring at the steering wheel for several minutes in a sort of paralyzed haze. One minute he had been running on his treadmill, wondering what he would cook for himself and Ashley that night. The next minute he was sitting outside of a police station, homeless. He could hardly believe that this whole ordeal was happening to him except for the fact that the word *Police* was lit up on the building façade in front of him, telling him undeniably that this was all true.

Now faced with the problem of finding shelter for the night, Tom pulled out his smartphone to see what a search for lodging would turn up. An establishment in the nearby town of Mount Kisco came up and when Tom dialed it a man with a hoarse voice answered. The rough sound made Thomas think of all the sad sacks he'd come across in life—the type that had been unpopular in high school and wound up in middle age still living at home with a gin-drinking, eighty-year-old mother and her five cats.

"We have one room left. With tax, it's $145 for a king bed," the man explained. Tom spelled his last name for the man and told him he'd be there soon.

"I can't reserve a room without a credit card number," the man tried to explain, but Tom had already hung up. He was more concerned that the room could book up in the twenty minutes or so it would take him to drive there and so he got on his way.

Tom was able to check in. Upon opening the door to his room for the night, Tom found himself surrounded by the scent of stale smoke and dog piss. A little trifold paperboard display from the motel chain's national headquarters sitting on the bureau had a no-smoking symbol displayed on it below a plume of swirls that represented fresh air. It was clear that renovations had not yet come to this location since the no-smoking policy had been put into place.

Tom missed his own bed already. He missed his daughter and his dog, Hercules, and the feel of his fleecy bathroom slippers on his feet as he, when home, walked to his sparkling clean home's bathroom sink to brush his teeth.

Once he had surveyed the motel room—taking in the dusty-rose-colored armchair and the bed covered with a patchwork quilt of powder blue and pink squares—Tom walked to the bathroom and put his car keys and his lone toothbrush down on the counter.

After looking in the mirror at his tired visage, he unwrapped the paper soap, splashed some water on his face to wash off the day's film, and then turned his intentions toward brushing his teeth. In all of his world travels, he always tried to find a way to brush. Yet, to Tom's surprise, he found that there was no toothpaste provided in this modest room. Tom experienced this as a sort of small injury on top of everything else that had occurred that day. It was almost humorous given what he had just gone through. Anyway, he was glad at least that the day was done and that he could settle in for some sleep to restore him for what lie ahead the following day. Sure, his mouth did not feel fresh and minty, but at least he was able to remove the plaque scum.

Soon, Tom stretched out on the bed on top of the covers and collected his phone so he could call Ashley and make sure she was okay.

"Not to worry, Dad, I'm fine," she told him when she answered. "I don't quite know what to do, but all's well here," she said.

And then, in an instant, Ashley's tone changed. "My God, what are you doing here?" she said in a loud and worried tone. "What are you doing here?"

Tom heard screaming in the background and started to panic. "Ashley, what's happening?" he asked.

"Satha just walked in and she's screaming at me 'Get out of here! You're not allowed here!'"

A whooshing sound moved across the phone, and Tom's nerves tightened as he imagined Satha getting physical with his daughter.

"Ashley, stay on the line," Tom said, "I'm calling the police."

Tom picked up the hotel phone and dialed 9-1-1 as quickly as his jittery fingers would allow. On the first nervous try, he hit 9-1-4, but then he hung up and hit 9-1-1 on the second try.

The 911 operator quickly transferred him to the North Castle Police Department, and Tom launched into his concerns. "There is a crazy woman in my house and she is accosting my daughter. She needs help. Your officers were there earlier this evening."

The police dispatcher tried to calm Thomas down. "Sir, we will be able to help you but we need some information from you first. Please try to speak more slowly," she said.

"You don't understand, my daughter needs help *right now*," Tom continued, irritated by the lack of urgency in the dispatcher's voice.

"Sir, I understand that, but I need the location of the incident and a description in order to send help. Please provide the street address and city name."

"I was just there at the police station. Sergeant Huffman knows exactly where the house is. He was there today. This is Thomas Strahan."

There was a long pause and then, "Hello, Mr. Strahan."

And for the first time since he had seen the officers shortly after five o'clock that day, Tom was suddenly glad that the police department was so small that the Sergeant himself was still there and had picked up the phone.

Even so, Sergeant Huffman's nonchalant, almost patronizing tone made him bristle. Tom felt like his head might pop off if someone didn't start showing some urgency. As he spoke to the Sergeant, he had Ashley on speaker and could still hear all manner of yelling and muffled movement happening at the Bedford home.

"Satha Naar is psychiatrically unstable, and she's shown up at my home and she is harassing or accosting my daughter. And if you don't go there immediately, I'm going back to make sure she is okay, protective order or not."

"No, no, don't do that, Mr. Strahan," Sergeant Huffman said. "You'll be in contempt, and we'd have to put you in jail. We'll be there. We'll be there quickly."

"Thank you, Sergeant. I'm very worried." Thomas hung up the hotel phone and returned to his cell phone.

"Ashley? Ashley?"

"Yeah, Dad, I'm here."

"What's going on now?" he asked.

"Satha is going crazy. She's throwing things around and keeps yelling at me and she's dragging Hercules out the front door."

"Go outside and wait—take Hercules, too," Tom told her. "The police will be there soon."

"Okay, but I'm very scared," she said. "You know how crazy Satha is."

Tom told Ashley that he would stay on the line with her until the police arrived.

The squad car arrived in ten minutes, fast enough to make Tom realize that they had been speeding on the winding country roads. He was grateful that during those ten minutes, Satha had not come outside to further harass Ashley and Hercules. But he hated to imagine what she was now doing inside the house with all of its contents to herself.

As soon as the police cars and their flashing lights arrived on the doorstep of 1 Smith Farm Road, Ashley told her father that they had arrived, and both father and daughter let out a sigh of relief. Tom began to calm ever so slightly. Tom allowed his daughter to get off of the phone line so she could speak to the police. As Tom would later learn from Ashley's debrief, Satha soon appeared on the doorstep in a plum satin bathrobe, as if she had been disturbed from sleep by an intruder and was now ready to tell the police about it. Her demeanor was curt and dictatorial, as if she had been seriously offended by poor customer service on the part of the police department. "This is my home," she blurted out, "and this young lady does not have my permission to be here." She lifted her chin in a quick nod to Ashley.

Ashley later told her dad that it had been eerie for her to see how quickly Satha could go from a screaming maniac to an offended, "pretend" sleepy homeowner. Tom imagined it must have been equally strange for the police to see how the presence of the tall, genteel, blue-eyed Mr. Strahan standing at that same front door just hours earlier had been replaced by that of the indignant, dark-haired Satha Naar. Her short stature was offset by her large presence that seemed to obliterate the fact that Thomas had ever lived there at all and, in fact, was the tenant-in-common owner of the property.

"Get her off the property immediately," Satha said in a stern and commanding voice. "I have to get up early tomorrow morning to commute to Columbia University, where my team and I are doing cancer research."

Ashley knew that she had every right to assert her place at the house that night. She had lived there with her father for over a year now and Satha knew that. But Ashley felt intimidated by the flashing lights on the one side of her and the stout, maniacal woman seething at her from the doorstep in her satin bathrobe. Ashley looked up at the police questioningly.

For the second time that night, Sergeant Huffman showed that the police officers did not know quite what to do. They had seen earlier that Ashley had been cooperative and the protective order did not say that Ashley or Hercules had to leave the house. However, they eventually concluded that, for their own safety, Ashley and Hercules should vacate the premises given this current development. Dr. Naar kept insisting that she would not allow Ashley back into the house. Although at that point, she was not screaming wildly as Mr. Strahan had indicated during his 911 call, Ashley reported that Satha had had a mean look in her eye that made the officers nervous.

"Is there some way you can get a ride someplace?" the police inquired of Ashley. "The protective order does not say that you have to leave, but it doesn't appear safe for you to stay here."

Seeing that the scales had tipped in her favor, Satha disappeared into the house and Ashley could hear the sound of her locking the front door.

"I could call my dad," Ashley said, "and he could come get me. He's staying at a motel in Mount Kisco tonight."

But Sergeant Huffman cut her off, reminding her that her father was not permitted to return to the house due to the protective order. Ashley scanned her mind for other ideas and tried to push away the vision of her sleeping at the police station that night. Then she thought of Natalie, her father's office assistant who lived in New Rochelle, about forty-five minutes away. Natalie wasn't like family, but she was all Ashley could think of under the circumstances.

Upon answering the telephone, Natalie did her best not to sound grumpy as she told Ashley that she could be there in forty-five minutes. Given that it was past ten o'clock at night, Natalie clearly considered this to be one of the stranger requests she had been asked to do as an assistant. However, she made sure to request recompense by adding it—at time and a half—to that month's invoice.

In the end, Natalie made it to the house in about an hour, as she'd had to take time to throw on a pair of jeans and a pair of black flats that she always kept by the front door. When she arrived at the Smith Farm Road house, she found Ashley and Hercules out on the front curb in front of the house. Ashley's head was slightly drooped, her eyes closed, and her left arm was wrapped around the waist of Hercules, who had sat down beside her to keep her company. Officer Scherf stood at attention nearby, while Sergeant Huffman spoke to someone on the police radio.

Natalie later reported that when she stepped out of the car to call to Ashley, she thought she saw a flicker of light in an upstairs window. But when she looked more closely, the gauzy curtains had fallen back into place, obscuring her view of the interior altogether. Natalie could not see Satha but imagined that she was inside somewhere, lurking and smirking.

Chapter 5

By the time Tom had to appear at the police station the next day, he had retained counsel and was feeling optimistic that he and one of his attorneys, Dan Shanahan, would be able to get this whole mess straightened out. The swirling upset of the night before had burned off, like a damp fog dispelled by the morning sun and Tom, having obtained a tube of toothpaste at the corner drugstore in Mount Kisco and taken a hot shower, was feeling like a much better version of himself. He had also been able to wash his workout clothes at the motel, and it helped too that the sun was shining outside and that the leaves of the trees arching alongside the road were twinkling in autumnal shades of orange, red, and yellow. The colors reminded Tom of one of the reasons why he had moved to New York from the West Coast in the first place: to enjoy a part of this beautiful country that he had never lived in before.

Tom met his attorney in the parking lot of the police station. Dan was dressed in a navy suit, white Oxford shirt, kelly-green-and-navy-striped tie, and penny loafers. Dan's dark hair sprouted thickly from his head like a lawn that had been seeded a bit too much, and he was red in the ears and cheeks as if he had just climbed a few too many flights of stairs. But his gigantic toothy smile showed that he was in good spirits and was a pleasant gentleman to be around. Tom gave Dan a warm handshake. Dan reciprocated with his own hearty squeeze.

"I typed up a short brief," Dan said, "which you are welcome to look over before we go in." He handed over a copy of the document in a chestnut-brown legal folder. Being an attorney himself, Tom started to mentally reword a few items, but he nodded with agreement as he read what Dan had prepared. He assessed that Dan and his team had indeed covered the essentials and in a rather expedient manner, given that they had just conversed on the topic by phone for the first time an hour and a half ago.

"This should be an open-and-shut matter given your background and the fact that no guns were even found on the premises," assured Dan. Tom felt likewise. He had been a good neighbor in his home of three years now, and there would be no record of the police ever having been called in to settle any disturbances, as he mostly kept to himself. Although Satha had done her share of screaming in the past few months as their business partnership dissolved and she moved out of the home they shared as tenants in common, Tom had managed to keep his cool and carry on. He had never thrown even a pencil in anger. Then, of course, there were his forty-plus years of service as an attorney, academician, and humanitarian for which he had received numerous awards and much recognition. Surely the Judge would be impressed when she learned of his background.

Dan opened one of the front doors of the police station and allowed Tom to enter first. In order to reach the courtroom from this side of the building, Tom and Dan had to pass by the door to the police agency. Inside, Tom saw Sergeant Huffman working at his desk. Tom took this as an opportunity to offer a warm hello and show Sergeant Huffman that he retained no hard feelings for yesterday's awkward events.

"Good morning, Sergeant!" Tom said in a generous tone. "Catch any criminals this morning?"

Sergeant Huffman smiled thinly, but his eyes darted back to his computer nervously, belying that something more than pleasantries was on his mind.

"Good morning, Mr. Strahan," he replied.

"Everything all right?" Tom asked, taking the paternal approach that came naturally to him now that he was a couple of decades or more older than the majority of people with whom he interacted every day.

"Well, sir, actually, we have a more serious problem now," the Sergeant said.

Tom and Dan moved a few paces closer to Sergeant Huffman's desk so they could have a more personal conversation.

"Really, what's that?" Tom asked.

"Guns have been located in the house," Sergeant Huffman explained.

Tom's brows rose in shock. "What?" he asked. "You fellows did a search last night and saw that there were no guns in the house."

"Well," Sergeant Huffman replied, "Dr. Naar called us today saying that guns were in the house."

"Where?" Tom interrupted, losing all sense of propriety as his heartbeat quickened.

"Well, we went out to the house this morning, and we found the guns on a low shelf in your closet in plain sight," Sergeant Huffman said. "There they were—all of those guns, just as you had described them."

"What?" Tom said. "If they were on a low shelf in my closet, the door of which had three years before been removed, it would have been impossible for Officer Scherf not to have seen them yesterday while conducting his search. I mean, this defies common sense and logic!"

Sergeant Huffman raised his hands as if to say, "Don't shoot the messenger."

"All I am telling you," Huffman added, "is what we saw and what we've taken into evidence."

Tom continued on with his argument, still not believing what he was hearing. "Would I have given consent to a search if I knew that guns were in the house? Would I have described the guns I own and which I believed to be out west in great detail if I had any inkling they were in my Bedford house? After all, I didn't fall off a turnip truck yesterday. Do you think I'm an absolute idiot? You'd already told me that you were looking for guns. Had I known guns were there, do you think I would have consented to a search? Especially with my background as one who's taught constitutional law for many years and who certainly knows that a search warrant is necessary if demanded?"

"All we can go on is what we saw, Mr. Strahan. We got out to the house this morning and there the guns were."

"So what next, then?" Tom asked.

"Well, Mr. Strahan, we have to place you under arrest, this time for contempt of court for not disclosing the guns and their location to us."

"My God, are you kidding me? This flies in the face of common sense!" Tom said, unable to keep his voice down. "You go out to the house yesterday while I'm there, do an exhaustive search looking for guns, and don't find them. Then, the next day, after I'm gone and once Ms. Naar is back on premises, you find guns. Don't you think it's possible that Ms. Naar or someone she hired placed the guns in the house? I mean, if they were in plain sight, as you say, I wouldn't have consented to a search and, consent or not, Officer Scherf would have seen them."

Sergeant Huffman, who had remained polite throughout this entire ordeal, did not lose his temper but simply answered with little emotion, "All we can go on is that we had a court order. We went out, exercised the order and, unlike what you represented, your unregistered guns were in the State of New York, County of Westchester, and you denied having knowledge of that."

Tom let out a small, sardonic laugh and said, "Of course, I denied it. I did not believe there were any guns on the premises or even in the state! And Officer Scherf saw for himself during an hour-long search that there were indeed no guns in the house. And even if there had been, so what? "Don't you realize that this doesn't pass the smell test? This should smell fishy to any experienced police officer."

"Well, at this time, we have to fingerprint you again, and our best fingerprint guy is here, so we should get started," Sergeant Huffman asserted. The Sergeant's politeness was now bleeding into an air of automaticity that niggled Tom greatly.

"Fine, fine, fingerprint me again," Tom said, and he looked at Dan to make sure he didn't have a different game plan. Dan nodded in agreement toward cooperation, and Tom asked where he should go next.

As Tom walked away from Sergeant Huffman's desk toward the room where he would be fingerprinted, he restrained himself from saying anything else as he didn't want to come across as belligerent and make the matter any worse. Still, he found himself foaming with anger as he mentally cursed Satha. How could she have so framed him? Where in the world did she find guns? He could just imagine her hiring someone to carry guns into the house or from wherever she had located them and place them in his closet for the police to see in irrefutable display. She would sometimes pick up day laborers, usually illegals, from town to do odd jobs and this might have been just one more odd job she had hired out.

But how had Satha gotten hold of his guns? Just as Tom had told the officers yesterday, he hadn't seen them in years and they were still out west—weren't they? Surely the guns she had placed inside the home she had obtained elsewhere. They couldn't be his—or could they?

The room where Tom's fingerprints were to be taken was painted sea-foam green and had bare walls except for one framed poster that hung behind a long formica table. On the poster, there was a regal-looking bald eagle perched on a branch in front of some distant snowcapped mountains, and the word LEADERSHIP appeared in big block letters beneath. Tom found himself gazing at the snowy mountains each of the seventeen times the officer took and retook his fingerprints.

It took a good hour and a half to conduct the procedure, and when it was complete, the officer concluded, "Well, we're not coming up with a match."

Dan, who had remained with Tom throughout the procedure, raised his brows in a look of victory.

Tom, in turn, was guileless with the officer and replied, "Well, even though I haven't seen the guns since 1999, I'd think my prints would be on them if, in fact, they are mine."

Then, he allowed himself to get straight to the heart of the matter. "But since my prints aren't on the guns, please use common sense. That means someone else had their hands on the guns and smudged my prints or removed them accidentally when carrying them into the house. Surely it's occurred to you that you should be taking the prints of Naar and interrogating her about how the guns magically appeared today when they weren't there last night." Tom continued, "This doesn't take police training, just common sense. First, one who fully understands his constitutional rights allows a consensual search of his premises.

The search was conducted and no guns were found. The next morning and after a mentally unstable woman had entered the house, the guns magically appear—and in plain sight. Now you tell me that my fingerprints can't even be found on any of the guns. So the logical question you should be asking yourselves is how could this happen? The next logical thing for any officer would be to interrogate Naar and to take her fingerprints, as she was the only person in the house between the nighttime search and the magical discovery of guns the next morning, an appearance only after she, and she alone, gained exclusive control of the premises. Again, when things don't add up, isn't it your obligation as police officers supposedly seeking justice to find out why?" concluded Tom.

The officer now looked disgruntled, as if he didn't like the way that Tom was talking to him or trying to do his job for him. Or perhaps the officer found the fact that Tom's story about why his fingerprints were not on the guns forward and brusque. Yet he could not deny that Tom's prints were not on the guns and that there had to be some reason for that.

Tom continued, "I ask again, why don't you take the fingerprints of this lady Naar, the one you refer to as 'Doctor,' to see if her fingerprints can be found on the gun?"

Sergeant Huffman replied: "Well, unless we have a court order to that effect, you know we won't be fingerprinting anyone else," he said. "If Judge Lysander wants us to take the prints of anyone else, she will tell us. Don't you understand that?"

"No, I don't understand that at all, since it defies common sense and basic police procedures under such circumstances. Your duty is to find the truth, not just to pass the buck and allow someone to be railroaded in an authoritarian way. That's not what our judicial system is all about. That's not what our country is all about. What it's about or should be about is to find and dispense justice, and that seems to be of no interest to this department and apparently to a Judge who's clearly in over her head," Tom concluded.

Regardless of the logic of what Tom had said, the fingerprint "expert" just shrugged his shoulders, unmoved by Tom's remarks, and waited for further instructions from Sgt. Huffman.

By this time, Tom didn't care whether the police or the Judge was angry. They were destroying the lives of several people and seemingly didn't give a shit. It was at that moment that Tom's eyes fell back upon the bald eagle in the poster with a bit of futile longing. It was becoming clearer and clearer to him that there was a great vacuum of knowledgeable leadership and/or experience in this police department and that he was going to need some great force of nature to swoop down and save him.

"I don't know what else to say," Tom went on, "except that if my fingerprints are on those guns, just match them up."

The fingerprint expert replied, "Look, I've already told you that we're trying to do just that and we're still not getting a match, but you admitted to Sgt. Huffman last night that the guns we've found fit the description of the ones you said belong to you. So apparently the confiscated guns are yours. That's enough for us."

"Well, it shouldn't be enough for you or any other officer. The fact that my fingerprints aren't there should speak volumes," Tom said as he folded his arms across his chest.

Unlike the fingerprinting officer, Sergeant Huffman appeared to more easily excuse Tom's sudden display of attitude, perhaps because the Sergeant had spent a good portion of yesterday with Tom and had no evidence to dispute that Tom was generally a good man. Still, the Sergeant seemed to operate from the position that the law was the law and the Judge's order was all that counted, regardless of the facts. Tom's weapons had been found at his home and were not registered in the County of Westchester.

There were consequences for that, according to the Sergeant.

"We'll have to leave this to the court to decide how to proceed," Sergeant Huffman finally declared. "Judge Lysander will be here in an hour or so and she can determine what is to be done next."

Although Sergeant Huffman had made this statement with little intonation, there was something scary about it to Tom. In fact, it was the lack of intonation that really frightened him. It was as if the Sergeant was either a highly sophisticated robot or an extremely unsophisticated human being who knew only how to obey orders without using independent thought to consider the circumstances.

"Well, then, I guess that my attorney and I will have to look forward to making my case before the Judge," Tom replied. "Surely, we can get this resolved. It's just pure, unadulterated nonsense and, as an experienced police offer, you should realize that."

"Perhaps so, Mr. Strahan," said Sergeant Huffman. "But we'll just have to wait and see. In a case like this, we just do what the Judge tells us to do."

Chapter 6

The sixty minutes that Tom was required to wait for Judge Lysander oozed slowly through the hourglass of time. Although he was typically an excellent and friendly conversationalist, Tom no longer felt like talking. He'd had his fill of the North Castle police and their sanitized politeness. His attorney, Dan, had returned to his legal office, saying he'd be back in an hour for the hearing. So Tom sat among a small bay of chairs in the waiting area, next to a coffee table and a pile of last year's magazines, and waited in silence for the Judge to appear. As he could not find a copy of the *New York Times* or anything else of interest to read, he just sat in a chair, crossing his left leg over his right and then his right leg over his left as his mind kept turning over the events that had occurred since he had been in the police station the night before.

Tom didn't like to curse and seldom did. Yet he found himself thinking about "that bitch Satha," how she had framed him in the most transparent way imaginable, and how the police were seemingly not disposed to do even a limited follow-up investigation. He hoped that Judge Lysander would be able to see through the veil of recent circumstances that had magically caused Tom's guns to show up in his home after he had been unlawfully removed from the premises. He told himself that she would surely act more logically than had her automaton police counterparts, who seemed to be doing no detective or investigative work on their own at all.

Finally, Judge Lysander arrived for another special court hearing on behalf of Tom, as this again was not seven o'clock at night nor was it one of her alternating Tuesdays. Tom and Dan entered the courtroom, sat alone in the front row of the otherwise empty courtroom, and awaited direction from the Judge. When she entered, she was wearing her black robe and the same corrective shoes from the evening before.

"Okay, Mr. Strahan, here we are again," she said. "The police have informed me that guns were found at your property early this morning and they match with specificity the ones you described to Sgt. Huffman last night.

"Mr. Strahan, as a result of your having unregistered guns in my jurisdiction and given that you denied having such guns on your property, the court is confiscating your weapons and issuing a protective order that forbids you from returning to your home or any part of the property at 1 Smith Farm Road for a year. You are also forbidden from leaving the state of New York during that time."

Tom's mouth fell open and he gasped in disbelief. "But your honor—" Tom started to say. However, he was immediately cut off by the Judge.

"Mr. Strahan, if you have anything to say, you will do it through your attorney. Anyway, I have the police report in front of me so I don't really want to hear anything else at this time. If this matter goes to trial, you'll have your opportunity to be heard."

All Tom wanted to say was that it was only after Naar had returned to the home that the guns had appeared, so Ms. Naar or someone she hired must have carried the guns into the home after he was removed by the police. There could be no other possible conclusion. But Judge Lysander hadn't finished speaking.

"Mr. Strahan, what I know is that these guns are yours—you've willingly admitted that—and it is you who will bear the consequences of keeping them without registering them in my county."

Neither Tom nor his attorney was given the chance to explain that the guns were licensed and properly registered in the state of California, where they had been gifted to him, and that he was not even aware that they had ever left the state of California.

But Judge Lysander was now gathering her papers, intent on ending the conversation as she announced that the hearing was over and anything else would have to be continued to her next scheduled courtroom session approximately ten days later.

Tom stood in the courtroom with Dan for five minutes longer after the Judge left. He was in disbelief over what he had just heard and observed. First, he was disturbed that Judge Lysander had not even considered the possibility that the guns were planted in his house. If they had been planted, then it showed that he did not willfully deny that the guns were in his home. It also pointed to the idea that the party lodging the complaint—Satha Naar—might be a person to investigate in order to get to the truth of what was going on.

Second, as punishment for having unregistered guns in the County of Westchester, the Judge had, in effect, taken away Tom's home and that of his daughter and also of their dog! And Judge Lysander had issued an order that he could not even return to his home for an entire year! Surely, the statute that declared it illegal to have unregistered guns in the County did not cite as possible punishment expropriation of one's home and all of one's possessions that were still in the home.

This was crazy: Tom had not been convicted of a crime, any crime. How could the Judge be meting out punishment? To make matters worse, she was doing so in a constitutionally unlawful way by dispossessing him of his property. In Tom's mind, this was a clear taking by the state in violation of the Fifth Amendment of the United States Constitution. "Has she any knowledge whatsoever of the Constitution?" thought Tom. The Fifth Amendment prevents the government from taking property without due process of law and without just compensation. "My Lord, hasn't she even heard of 'the presumption of innocence'? What kind of kangaroo court is this?" Tom thought. She still hadn't even arraigned him on any charge whatsoever, let alone given him a full hearing.

On top of all this, Tom was forbidden to leave New York: In effect, he had become a prisoner of the State. A mandate like this was made all the more ridiculous by the fact that in this part of New York, the roads tended to wind in and out of neighboring Connecticut as often as bees pollinated flowers in springtime. Given the Judge's irrational order, Tom would not even be able to drive or take the Metro-North train to New York City to visit his daughter, if she was able to find a place to stay there, without crossing into and out of Connecticut. In fact, he couldn't even drive to his doctor's office!

Finally, as the Judge and the bailiff had vacated the room, making it painfully clear that the court hearing was over, Tom and Dan walked out of the courtroom together. Tom, stunned, almost seemed to drag his feet along the linoleum floor. With his mind filled with confusion and anger, he had lost some of the progress he had made in teaching himself to walk again since his car accident.

Tom wasn't quite sure what to do with himself, so he and Dan decided to have a cup of coffee together and discuss what they should next do. Anything was better than staying in the toxic environment of the nondescript courtroom and the adjacent police station.

Dan and Tom went to the nearby Street Car Diner, whose interior walls were covered with authentic vintage Pepsi-Cola posters as well as framed and signed photographs of various celebrities who had dined there. The photos included images of Richard Gere, Martha Stewart, Glenn Close, Bill and Hillary Clinton, and many others who either lived in the area or had simply passed through. Over coffee, Dan and Tom talked about the court order that had just been handed down.

Tom started by asking, "Who is this Judge Lysander and does she know anything about the law or the Constitution?"

Dan replied, "Actually, she is a practicing attorney In the area, although she's not highly rated by the various attorney rating services. Here in New York, there are over three thousand of these part-time justices sitting in small hamlets or villages throughout the state. In fact, it's not even necessary that one be an attorney or to have any training in law to serve as a village Judge. No doubt about it, we have a strange court system in this state. First, we have a Court of Appeals. This would be the equivalent of the Supreme

Court in the other states. Then we have the appellate division of the Court of Appeals. Below that is the Supreme Court, the equivalent of the Superior Court in most states. Then come county courts and, after that, specialized courts. Then we have city courts in our larger cities. At the bottom of the totem pole we have what we call "inferior courts." That's what we are dealing with here. They are usually located in tiny villages such as the one here in Armonk. In fact, we have close to forty of them just in this one county alone, and there are scores of counties in the state. These courts generally handle small claims matters not to exceed $3,000, cases involving traffic tickets, and local zoning matters—not much else. So here we are talking about the bottom of the food chain, if you get the analogy. That's why people like Lysander are simply elected with or without judicial qualifications," concluded Dan.

"Don't they at least have to be found qualified by some sort of judicial qualifications committee?" asked Tom.

"No, I'm afraid not. Most of those who happen to be attorneys do not have very active or successful practices and just want to supplement their income stream with a soft job that comes with health care and pension benefits, as well as other perks of office. Others just want the prestige of being called 'Judge' or 'Your Honor.' I've got to tell you, when I told Judge Lysander in chambers about your background, I could tell that she initially felt intimidated. My suspicion now is that she's determined to demonstrate her power, bottom of the food chain or not," Dan concluded.

"How do these people get elected?" asked Tom.

"Just like any other politician. Some inherit a well-known name in the area where they live, some have independent wealth that allows them to buy name recognition, and some just scratch around for money from special interests such as insurance companies, trial lawyers, and so on. Most seek endorsements from local law enforcement agencies. I do know that here in Armonk, the police officers are closely tied to Lysander. It's rumored that she's had some problems of her own in the past, but I've never delved into that and I don't intend to. After all, although I don't appear in inferior courts very often, I do practice in this county, and the various courts and agencies go out of their way to protect one another. Anyway, the word is that if you want to do something in this village, the best place to start is with Lysander. I'm sure there's mutual back-scratching of one sort or another going on. After all, we are talking about New York politics, and I'm sure you know something about the history of politics in this state."

"OK, I accept that the system smells to high heaven, but where will I go given Lysander's actions today?" Tom asked, as he processed the fact that his home was suddenly off limits to him not just for a night but now for an entire year. His beautiful home was a major part of the reason he'd moved east to New York in the first place. Tom found the land on the Bedford property to be quite spiritual. There were several acres for his dog to roam on, and Tom had cleared forested paths that he could hike when he wanted to commune with nature. A lifetime of hiking, mountain biking, kayaking, and more attested to his wish to not be far from nature for long. Nature was his cathedral, not a 1970s-vintage motel like the one he had stayed in the night before. And although he had made a handful of friends in the area since moving to New York, there was no one he could comfortably ask to allow him and his dog to move in with, and certainly not for twelve months!

What was he to do?

Dan grabbed a napkin and quickly wrote down the name of a few other motels and hotels for Tom to consider while Tom's mind struggled with his dilemma, mulling it over and over like the spot on someone's gums where a tooth has just been lost. As he did so, he kept discovering additional nuances among the raw tenderness of the situation, such as the fact that not only had he, his daughter, and their family dog been evicted from their home but that he was also forbidden from returning there even to gather his belongings, and almost everything of value in the house was his. There also remained common items not of great value, such as his undershirts and shorts; his suits, sport coats, and dress pants; his reading glasses; and so on. But there were also personal items and family heirlooms, such as his leather-bound daily journal, his familial and personal artifacts and antiquities, his financial and work papers, his computers and the external hard drive in which he kept his files backed up, his address book of over 20 years, and the neat pile of bills that he paid on the first of each month. There was also his deceased mother's jewelry, including the white gold and sapphire ring that he had already wrapped and left in his nightstand in preparation for his daughter's birthday. All that and many other items of value were still in the house. There were also the boxes that John had shipped to him in the camper and that had never been opened— by him, that is.

Clearly, the guns were also gone. Although Tom had no intention of ever firing them again absent a need to defend himself, it pained him to think of no longer having those gifted mementos from some of the finest years of his career. The police would probably be required by law to destroy such weapons upon seizing them. But Tom was all too familiar with the common police practice of officers keeping guns of value for their private collections, especially ones that had seldom, if ever, been fired. It was strange that after all he had done to help Satha, the sum of his sour experiences with her could be captured in the way she had obviously located his guns and placed them in such a way that she could vindictively have him framed. After all, by this time, he had learned bit by bit that she'd had a lifetime of criminal conduct, so why should he now be surprised?

After all, Satha was the kind of woman who tried to squeeze juice from everything she touched, so it was rather fitting that in finding Tom's guns, she had leveraged them for an outcome that suited her just perfectly. Those conveniently discovered guns had allowed her to return to the home in which she had a partial interest while also hitting him with a black eye that she, no doubt, thought would get him to drop his suit against her. What a sick and horrible human being!

As bad as things were, shortly thereafter Tom was contacted by his attorney saying that Naar had now filed yet another complaint based on the same facts with the Family Law Court, an arm of the Supreme Court in White Plains, New York, and that Tom would have to make an appearance there as well. On the date of the Supreme Court hearing, held before a Judge Whitehall, both Naar and her attorney were chastised by the Court. Judge Whitehall held that Naar lacked "standing" to even have brought the matter before him since Naar and Strahan were not married and did not even co-habit in the traditional use of the phrase. Moreover, as the Court pointed out, Naar had never, by her own admission, been threatened by Tom, had never even seen the guns in question and, if they were in the house, did not even have any idea where they might be.

Thus, Judge Whitehall dismissed the complaint, said that a Protective Order would be entirely inappropriate under the circumstances, and admonished Naar and her attorney to not again abuse the Judicial process in what appeared to be a blatant attempt to gain some sort of leverage over Tom.

Tom left the large and impressive Supreme Court Building in White Plains feeling a great sense of relief since the Supreme Court ruling would presumably be binding on any action taken or to be taken by the inferior court in Armonk. His attorney felt likewise. He said that he would bring Judge Whitehall's ruling to the immediate attention of Judge Lysander and that this entire matter should now be concluded. Tom felt a renewed sense of justice but, as things developed, that feeling was misplaced.

The following day Dan called Tom and said that Lysander had taken the position that she was not bound by Judge Whitehall's ruling. "That's insane," replied Tom. "Our entire system of justice is based on judicial precedent and you've already explained that the Supreme Court stands well above any of the inferior courts in New York such as the Justice court in Armonk."

Dan responded: "That's correct for the most part, but we have another strange twist to our court system in New York. There isn't always a direct vertical line from our highest court down to the lowest court, in this case the one in Armonk. Lysander's position is that she isn't bound by the Family Court ruling since that is, to use her expression, a quasi-independent arm of the Supreme Court. Technically, she may be right, but her position is totally bizarre and completely unheard of. Boy, she really has a thorn up her butt for reasons I can't imagine. You've certainly been polite and deferential in her presence. Quite frankly, she seems to be taking umbrage that anyone, even a higher Judge, would intrude on her little Judicial domain. We'll just have to see what happens next. Again, for some undisclosed reason, she seems to have some kind of vested interest in your matter Tom, though I can't even imagine what it might be."

Chapter 7

With the experience and insight that came from living a life of amazing highs and low lows, Tom now sensed that he might be dipping into another downward spiral. The last bad stretch had occurred eleven years ago, the year his older brother, Leon, was diagnosed with a rare form of cancer called Merkel cell carcinoma. Tom and Leon were very close, and Tom was determined to see if he could uncover an alternative modality for the treatment of Leon's cancer. Leon's own medical team had told him that there were no known cures for this condition and that he should expect to die in a matter of months.

Never one to settle for no and unfazed by travel, Tom embarked on a worldwide circuit in pursuit of a cure. He first traveled to Montreux, Switzerland, a noted medical center. He then went to London and thereafter to Mexico, where he conferred with American-trained physicians conducting cancer research that they could not conduct in the United States. Finally, he visited one of the top research and treatment centers in the country, the renowned University of Texas MD Anderson Cancer Center in Houston. At each place, Tom was informed that there was no known cure for Merkel cell carcinoma or even a treatment that the physicians could offer. Only Dr. Venkat Aggarwal at the MD Anderson Cancer Center could provide Tom with some small hope.

"I've been speaking by phone to an epidemiologist named Dr. Satha Naar at the Mailman School of Public Health at Columbia University in New York City who tells me that she is working on trying to address different types of chronic disease, but especially cancer," Dr. Aggarwal said. "Dr. Naar has apparently determined, as has my team, that the underlying cause of almost all chronic illness and disease is inflammation. She has also found that, especially in connection with the incidence of cancer, the rates are much lower in India and other parts of South and Southeast Asia than in North America, which has the highest incidence in the world."

Tom kept his gaze fixed on Dr. Aggarwal, who spoke in a steady and clear voice.

"And yet those same people who have a low incidence of cancer in their own countries," Dr. Aggarwal continued, "when they come to the United States, their incidence goes right up and matches that of Caucasians, African Americans, and Hispanics. Dr. Naar tells me that she has concluded, as have we, that it is possible—in fact probable—that cancer has something to do with the nature of a person's diet."

Dr. Aggarwal went on to explain how Dr. Naar had begun to do extensive research on this topic, with a specific look at curcumin, a key ingredient in the spice turmeric which is commonly used in South Asian cuisine.

"Our team of twelve here is doing similar research," Dr. Aggarwal explained, "but Dr. Naar may well be ahead of us. She is certainly familiar with our studies and she has called me many times. You may want to go to New York and speak to her. We do not yet have anything here that can help your brother, but I believe that Dr. Naar may be looking to start a human trial."

It was a long shot, Tom knew, but maybe there was something to it. Dr. Aggarwal put him in touch with Dr. Naar by phone, and Tom purchased a plane ticket to New York City, wondering if something of promise might actually await him there.

The first time that Tom met Dr. Naar, she was sitting on a wide stone bench in the Van Am Quad of Columbia University's campus, wearing a white lab coat and with a stethoscope hanging loosely around her neck. Because Columbia has a large and busy campus, Dr. Naar had suggested they meet at that popular outdoor spot during her lunch break from her research and teaching work at the Mailman School of Public Health.

Upon first seeing each other on the quad, it took a moment for the two of them to identify each other. After they had confirmed that Tom was Tom and Dr. Naar was Dr. Naar, they smiled and shook hands.

"Pleased to meet you, Dr. Naar," Tom said. He tried to be as warm and polite as he could, but given his concern over his brother's diagnosis, he could not conceal the edge of stress in his voice.

"It's a pleasure to meet you as well," Dr. Naar returned. Although quite a bit overweight, she had a pleasant face and warm brown eyes, and she spoke with a mild Indian British accent that she had retained from living in Singapore for most of her life while being raised by her ethnically Indian parents. Her thick black hair fell relatively straight behind her shoulders, a stark contrast to her white lab coat in terms of its color, but everything about her seemed to go well

73

together, from the simple silver hoop earrings she wore to the tasteful application of lipstick.

"Thanks for taking the time to meet me, and on such short notice," Tom said. "Dr. Aggarwal speaks highly of you."

"My pleasure," Dr. Naar said. "I know it can be hard when you are fighting for a loved one."

"Thank you," Tom said, touched by Dr. Naar's apparent sensitivity.

The two took a few moments to get acquainted, and then Dr. Naar suggested that they go to lunch.

"Do you mind if my husband joins us?" she asked.

"Not at all," Tom said. "I would be delighted."

When Dr. Naar stood, Tom could see she was rather short in terms of height, but her stature was nonetheless sturdy, with broad shoulders and a thick and rather heavy upper body. Tom, who stood almost a foot taller than Dr. Naar and looked slender in his navy suit, followed her lead as they walked off the university campus and down Amsterdam Avenue. They ended up at an Indian restaurant, where Dr. Naar's husband was indeed waiting for them. When Tom asked Dr. Naar's husband, Gopal, what he did for a living, he explained that he was an executive with IBM who had been transferred several years earlier from Singapore to IBM headquarters in nearby Westchester County.

"And the U.S. government at that time granted me a work visa due to my credentials as a highly educated research scientist," said Dr. Naar.

Once the three of them had ordered their food and received some samosas and aloo papri chaat as starters, Tom told Dr. Naar that he was anxious to hear more about her research.

"It's really very exciting," she said. "We began by looking at the effects of injecting curcumin in lab animals and in the process found that these animals were experiencing significantly better rates of recovery from a number of diseases and maladies when compared to those that had not been treated with curcumin."

Tom continued to listen to Dr. Naar as he scooped some aloo papri chaat onto his plate.

"But curcumin is not the only substance we've been looking at. We've found a handful of other natural substances that seem to reduce chronic inflammation in the body and to be therapeutic and efficacious in treating certain maladies in rats. Examples are heart disease, restless leg syndrome, Lyme disease and—most significantly—cancer. I've developed a supplement that contains all of these items and we have already started using it with human subjects. If your brother is interested, we could provide him with a trial supply," said Dr. Naar. "It's completely natural and homeopathic, so there's no concern about side effects or damage to the body as you have with the various and more traditional pharmaceuticals."

"Knowing what you do, Dr. Naar, do you think my brother might be a good candidate for the supplement?" Tom asked. "He's Stage 4 and it's merkel cell carcinoma, which every skilled medical person I've spoken to has told me does not respond to existing treatments."

"We have had some magnificent results with our supplement in our human research participants," Dr. Naar responded, "although none of them has your brother's condition. Also, he's in an advanced stage so we can't know for certain if this will work for him. Nonetheless, given what I've seen so far with the supplement I think it's worth a try."

Tom proceeded to ask Dr. Naar a number of questions, and each she answered with a detailed medical explanation that Tom was able to follow with relative ease. Given his years of experience wading through long legal documents, Tom was good at synthesizing conclusions from a series of technical points. Everything Dr. Naar shared with him made sense, such as how she and her team believed the supplement worked to reduce the cancer in their lab animals. Her team's research appeared to be completely in sync with the research that Dr. Aggarwal and his team were doing at MD Anderson, and Tom was certainly intrigued.

Although Leon was not enrolled in a clinical trial, within a week's time Dr. Naar had sent a large sample of the supplement to Leon's address, which Tom had provided to her. Along with the supplement, she sent typed instructions on how and when to take it. She also explained that it would take some time for the effects of the supplement to be evidenced, so it was important to be consistent and patient with the treatment.

"You know, I've got my own doctors," Leon had said to Tom after his arrival back in California to deliver the news of his worldwide visits to medical and research facilities. "And they recommend nothing other than chemotherapy and radiation," said Leon.

Nonetheless, Leon agreed to give the supplement a try. However, he had far less hope for the supplements than did Tom, in part because he had not met Dr. Naar himself and in part because he never was much of a believer in alternative treatments. Still, it made Leon happy to do something that put Tom at ease, and he hoped that his own skepticism would be proven wrong and that they would indeed see improvements in his condition.

Once the supplementation had begun, Tom called Leon every few days to see how things were going and was touched to learn that Dr. Naar was checking in on Leon as well by e-mailing him daily to see how he was doing with the supplements and the cancer in general. It was really admirable to Tom that Dr. Naar was willing to give that kind of personal attention to his brother and that she found time to reach out amid what surely were her busy days. When receiving a "thank you" phone call from Tom for being helpful to his brother, Dr. Naar humbly said, "It is nothing. Of course I am happy to do it." Tom, who valued kindness and integrity above many other things, did not forget how Dr. Naar had been willing to make time for his brother.

Sadly, the trial therapy could not in the end save Leon. Within just a few weeks, the already advanced merkel cell carcinoma had overtaken his body and he was laid to rest in San Diego, California in April 2002. They were never able to determine whether Dr. Naar's supplement had had a positive effect on him as not enough time had elapsed to measure it.

Tom's mother also died a few months later of what her doctors deemed a broken heart. Shortly thereafter, Tom's wife of over thirty-five years served him with divorce papers and, on the day he was supposed to attend a birthday party for the son of his oldest daughter, a delivery truck struck him as he exited a card store. The year 2002 was indeed a very bad year for Thomas Strahan, and he hoped he would never have to go through something like that again.

Chapter 8

Tom did not see Dr. Naar again for over four years.

It was an unusually warm day in October 2006 when she phoned him at his home out West to invite him to come to New York to see the business she was about to launch to sell the supplement line to the public.

"I have a company that, with help, will soon be up and running, and it's all based on my research," Dr. Naar said. "But I need someone with knowledge of business to assist me. Is there any time when you might be in New York again that we could meet? I'd love to get some insight from you."

Tom replied that, by coincidence, he already had plans to be in New York City in a couple of weeks. He was the international chair of a global nonprofit and they were considering moving their headquarters from the West Coast to either New York City or Washington, D.C. Tom would be assessing the options during his upcoming trip to the east coast.

"We could probably arrange a meeting while I'm in the city," Tom said. He didn't imagine he'd want to get heavily involved with Dr. Naar's new enterprise, and yet he was intrigued with her progress and was certainly willing to lend an ear.

Although the supplement had come too late to help his brother, Tom still felt optimistic about its potential to help others on the basis of everything he knew to date. Dr. Naar had called him about once a year after his brother's death to update him on her positive strides with the research, and Tom could still remember compelling details from the extensive PowerPoint slide presentations he had been shown by Dr. Aggarwal's research team in Houston.

"That's wonderful," Dr. Naar replied. "Send me your travel arrangements and we'll find a time to meet."

Tom made a note on his legal pad to get back to Dr. Naar with his trip details, and he listened as she went on to share other news, including that she and her husband had gotten a divorce. Tom thought little of this announcement other than that he was sincerely sorry for the couple. Having himself gone through divorce, he knew how painful it could be.

"I'm sorry to hear that," Tom replied, although Dr. Naar seemed fairly oblivious to his comment, replying that Gopal had been a very bad husband and it was good to finally be away from him. It was very difficult financially, she said, but at least she did not have to suffer from his verbal and physical abuse anymore.

Two weeks later, Dr. Naar picked Tom up from Kennedy Airport in an SUV. "All set to head to Bedford?" she asked after they had said their hello's and Tom had loaded a briefcase and a black duffel bag into the backseat.

"Yes indeed, Dr. Naar," Tom replied cordially, looking forward to the small adventure of visiting

Westchester County, as he had not had occasion to visit that part of New York State before.

Dr. Naar told him that he should call her Satha, and Tom agreed to do so as it seemed that they were on their way to being friends. To be clear, Tom had no romantic interest in Satha. She had a pleasant face and was seemingly quite intelligent, but Tom felt no chemistry toward her in that way. Instead, he respected her for the dedication she seemed to show to her research and the tenacity she displayed in wanting to build her commercial business.

As the two of them pulled into the long driveway of the home in Bedford, Satha explained how she had obtained ownership of the house as a result of her divorce from Gopal. "It's not been easy to hold on to, though," she confessed as she cranked the parking brake and turned off the ignition. "Not on a professor's salary."

"I can see why you'd want to try," Tom said as he stepped out of the SUV and took in the property. "May we walk the grounds a bit?" he asked.

"Of course," Satha said. "Let me change my shoes into something better for walking, and I'll show you around."

In a short while, they were back outside, meandering the five acres of the home's grounds. Beyond the generous parcel of flat land upon which the large house itself was situated, there extended a gentle upward slope that was dotted with green ground cover and gray and black boulders. There was also a smattering of trees, from large oaks and river spruce to smaller understory trees like dogwoods and American redbuds. Autumn had struck recently, so the leaves of the trees shone in brilliant shades of red, orange, plum, and yellow and littered the ground with a festive sprinkling of their colors as well.

Satha and Tom followed a path alongside a trickling stream coming down the hillside until it led them past some great rock outcroppings to trails above. Once there, Tom took a deep breath of the crisp, cold air and marveled at the surroundings. He could see the blue sky above as well as the shimmering leaves of the autumn trees below. In the distance, there was a rock amphitheater, and Satha explained how she and Gopal had found some Native American artifacts on their property when a crew they hired was digging to lay a foundation for a spacious gazebo that overlooked the property and house below.

So beautiful and peaceful was the view from there that Tom could have easily sat at the top of the ridge for a couple of hours, reflecting or meditating. But alas, time did not allow for it, and so he followed Satha back down the trails after she had sufficiently shown him around.

Once inside the house, Satha and Tom warmed their hands over two steaming cups of coffee made by Satha's assistant, Lisa Yang, with whom Tom was immediately impressed. Satha then proceeded to give Tom a tour of the lower level of the home, where she had set up the company for the moment. Lisa sat typing on a computer at a desk next to a black filing cabinet, and Satha stepped inside her own office to show Tom a few samples of the product.

"We've got several cases in the garage," she explained, "but this is the current packaging. As you can see, it is really quite plain, so this is one of the areas where I could use help. My specialty is in the formulations—you know, the clinical side of things. But

I really don't know how best to market a product or win customers."

Tom could see that the simple white-and-blue label with a few lines of bold text on it could use some spiffing up as he opened a bottle to take a peek inside. Past the paper covering, he observed the deep saffron-colored powder that filled the bottle.

"Be careful you don't get any of that on your clothes," Dr. Naar warned. "You won't be able to get the stain out."

Nevertheless, Tom poured some into his palm to take a closer look and then sniffed the yellowish-orange powder. The powder gave off a very earthy curry smell, quite powerful, and Tom felt a pang of sadness that this product had not been able to help his brother. But might it have helped if it had been introduced to Leon earlier? Perhaps not, but who could know?

As Satha removed the supplement bottle from his hand, she replaced it with a book. "Here, this is for you," she said, as she gave him a slim paperback book with her photo on it. "It's a publication of mine and you should take a look at it when you have time, maybe on the flight home. It will give you more details on the effectiveness of the supplement line along with conclusions from the research we've done at the university."

"Thanks," Tom said politely, giving the book a quick skim and then tucking it under his arm.

As the two of them finished the tour of the lower level of the home, Tom discovered another office where a second party could work on the business as it grew. There was also room for recreation down there, with a pool table and exercise equipment already spread out among the remaining square footage—

perhaps a vestige of when Gopal had lived there and the couple had used the ground level as part of their home. It just appeared to be collecting dust at the moment and Satha, being quite overweight, certainly didn't appear to be a fitness buff.

The rest of the home, although sparsely furnished, was quite auspicious in terms of sheer size and architectural detail. It had three stories and contained nineteen different rooms, including six bathrooms. There were high ceilings, a massive fireplace, pine floors, marble bathrooms, granite countertops, and a grand staircase that divided the home into two separate wings.

Before the end of the visit, Satha showed Tom to the three-car garage where she stored her extra supplies of supplement. Numerous cardboard shipping boxes were piled high on a spot where a single car could have been parked and Satha explained how this was her third installment of the supplement since she had opened shop.

"I only hope I can keep things going as successfully as they have been so far. We've filled initial demand, but I know I need the help of someone with a business background to spread the word, secure for us some large contracts, and get us on the shelves of Whole Foods, Mrs. Green's, Trader Joe's, and other such stores," continued Satha.

She seemed to be almost pleading. However, Tom thought better than to offer his own services in any full-time capacity given how busy he was with his humanitarian travel and writing and the nonprofit that he led. But he did let Satha know that he would try to make himself available in the coming months if she wanted to stay in touch by phone.

"You may be onto something, Satha," he said, "and I would like to be around to see if you succeed." Tom wondered, could something as simple as the ingestion of natural supplements really do what the pharmaceutical companies had been unable to do after decades of research and development?

Chapter 9

"You could move here, into this home," Satha suggested to Tom the next time they met in person in Bedford. "The house is huge and you could have your own wing, and then you'd be right on site so we could launch the business together."

It was 2007 and Tom was in New York again making further assessments as to where his global nonprofit would be relocated: Washington, D.C. or New York City. Satha had arranged another meeting with him to further discuss her business launch. She was dogged in her efforts to get Tom to join her in the company, and although he was not actively seeking an investment opportunity, he felt intrigued by her offer given the potential for the supplement to help so many people.

"It's a huge house and I can't keep it on my own," Satha continued. "Gopal isn't giving me a penny of support and I'm stretched to the max paying for the mortgage, upkeep, and bills, not to mention expenses related to my kids' college."

Tom paused to think about the offer but said nothing, as he really didn't know where he stood on the issue and wanted to hear what else Satha had to say.

"I'll give you half ownership in the business and in the house if you agree to join me as a business partner and to help me keep the property up," she said next.

Tom considered Satha's generous offer. Half ownership in the property was certainly enticing. Valued at up to three million dollars based on the appraisal Satha showed him, the property certainly had the potential to contribute significantly to Tom's portfolio of investments. And with its rugged, natural landscaping, the property was more than beautiful. It seemed to be somewhat spiritual to Tom, with its preponderance of natural light and exhaustive granite outcroppings. It would make for some amazing roaming grounds for Hercules, Tom's dog, and Tom had been looking about for a new place to live anyway. The rental lease on his home out west was going to expire at the end of the year. He could find another place in the west, but given that he'd be working in New York and Washington, D.C. due to the relocation of the nonprofit that he chaired, it seemed to make sense for him to head east.

Besides, Tom had never lived on the east coast, and this could be a unique opportunity for him to get to know the area better. He could live in proximity to Manhattan while avoiding the hubbub and fray of the actual city itself. He was no longer married either, and his youngest daughter, Ashley, was in college. Thus, Tom was free to live wherever he wanted. If it didn't work out in Bedford, nothing would be lost. He could simply move out and begin again elsewhere. Change and adventure had never bothered him.

Tom thought too about the painful loss of his brother, Leon. He thought about all of the lives and families touched by cancer in America and around the world. He wondered if he was standing at a place in his life where things were purposefully coalescing around him. He wondered if he was being called to bring this supplement to more people—and, if so, should he be listening?

"What do you think?" Satha pressed.

Tom cleared his throat and went for it. "Okay, I'm willing to give it a try," he said. "If it doesn't work out, it doesn't work out," he thought.

"That's marvelous!" Satha said as she clapped her hands together and smiled. She looked as happy as if she had won a tennis match at Wimbledon.

In the weeks following Tom's decision to move east and become a co-owner in the Quintessence of Life business and of the property in Bedford, Satha had her attorney draw up the necessary legal documents and saw that those pertaining to the house were properly recorded. Tom could be a fifty–fifty partner with Satha in the business, and he would be a tenant-in-common owner of the house. However, insofar as the business was concerned, Tom recommended that Satha's interest be 50.5% and his 49.5% so that they could take advantage of the company being minority controlled.

Satha signed all of the paperwork that her attorney prepared, and Tom noted a renewed sense of enthusiasm in her voice whenever they spoke. It reminded him of the way she had seemed when he had first met her in the quad at Columbia University in 2002, when she and Gopal were still married. Back then, she had appeared to be full of unadulterated optimism and hope, before financial times had gotten tough for her.

Although her optimism had seemed perfectly normal then, after Tom returned west to clear up pending matters there and prepare for the move east, he began to notice that Satha's optimism sometimes veered into a certain overzealousness. Satha started calling Tom on a daily basis. While Tom had really warmed to the idea of helping to launch Quintessence of Life, he had to admit that the frequent phone calls from Satha were a bit much. Having spent the first portion of his life without electricity, a telephone, or running water, he had never fully embraced modern technology, the phone included. In addition, given his somewhat stoic personality, he simply didn't feel the need to waste time with idle chitchat. He would listen to Satha drone on for as long as he could and then inform her that he had another obligation and would get off the line.

As Tom finalized his plans to move to Bedford, Satha offered to fly out west to help him drive some of his things across the country. Tom let her know that he could handle everything himself, but Satha insisted that the least she could do was help him with the driving. So Tom finally agreed to accept her help. Tom hired a moving company to take furniture and other heavy items east.

On the day of his departure, he loaded up his car with Satha, who had flown in from New York; his dog, Hercules; and whatever of Tom's essential belongings he could fit into his car. He also brought his laptop, a suitcase full of clothes, a tennis racket, food and other necessities for Hercules, and not much else due to the lack of space.

What he left out west included his array of sporting and camping equipment, several pieces of artwork, his gun collection, ten boxes of books, several photo albums, a super deluxe road camper, most of his business equipment, and a few pieces of furniture. Some of these items were still in the attic of the home where his ex-wife continued to reside after their divorce, while the other items Tom stored at his friend John's house in Encino, California. If things went well in Bedford, Tom would eventually send for these other belongings and also have them brought east.

The first several hours of the drive went smoothly. Traffic was light and Tom and Satha were making good progress. It wasn't until most of the way through Nevada that Tom asked Satha if she'd like to take the wheel for a while. They filled up on fuel and grabbed some snacks from the convenience store, and then Tom settled into the passenger seat to stretch his legs and relax while Satha took a turn at driving.

Unfortunately, no relaxation was to be had, as Tom discovered that Satha had minimal control over the vehicle. One minute, she was riding the center dividing line, crossing into the lane of oncoming traffic; the next, she was careening toward the shoulder, where she would then continue to drive on the far right rather than staying in her proper lane. She would speed the car up and then slow it down, never settling on a consistent speed.

"Why are you doing that?" Tom asked at one point.

Satha explained, "I can't go over the speed limit because I've had wrecks before."

"Well, just go a steady speed then," Tom suggested.

"I don't know how to do that," Satha confessed, and Tom couldn't help but say that it was pretty easy to do so.

"You can actually put it on automatic control if you want," he said.

"No, that scares me!" Satha shared and continued to alternate accelerating and decelerating her speed. Thus, the car was jerking its way down the road as it weaved from left to right until Tom couldn't take it anymore.

"Well, pull over then," Tom commanded in a firm voice. He needed to get Satha out of the driver's seat before they got pulled over or, worse, got into another one of her wrecks.

Chapter 10

In five days' time and in spite of horrendous winter weather and driving conditions, especially going through Wyoming and Nebraska, Tom pulled his car into the long driveway of the home in Bedford. The grounds were as magnificent as he had remembered, and Hercules launched off to explore the forested groves and hillsides as soon as the car doors opened. It was still wintertime, and once he had made some headway through the snow and into the yard, the gentle Weimaraner sniffed the trails leading up to the rock outcroppings as Tom unpacked the car and Satha disappeared inside to check on the house.

When the car was finally empty, save for a few food wrappers and empty water bottles, Tom called Hercules to him. They sat on the front step so Tom could pet his lovable companion and they could take in the scenery together. As Tom took a deep breath in, he smelled a scent that reminded Tom that he was in a new part of the country.

"Hercules," Tom said, running his fingers over the dog's grayish coat, "we have embarked on a new adventure."

Hercules gave a low, happy groan, and Tom gave him a few strokes on the top of his head between his ears and then a few more gentle strokes under the dog's chin. Tom had watched many friends and loved ones depart over the years—his brother, his mother, his father, and friends who had encountered health problems or misfortune—but Hercules had remained by his side unrelentingly through thick and thin. The only time the two had been separated for any great length since first coming together was during the six months or so that Tom was recovering from the car accident and could not return to his own home. Hercules had been left behind there to eventually stay with John, one of Tom's closest friends.

Tom could still remember the way Hercules had greeted him with total joy on the day they were reunited—with excited licks and a short-docked Weimaraner wagging tail. Although Hercules couldn't speak with words, the way he had faithfully followed Tom from room to room for the following week had spoken volumes.

Hercules and Tom had been through a lot together, and now they were about to embark on a new chapter of their lives, one that promised to be good. The global nonprofit that Tom chaired had ultimately decided to relocate to Washington, D.C. which Tom could access with ease by train. He looked forward to discovering how the headquarters might thrive in the new location at the heart of the nation's government, where so many international nonprofit organizations were headquartered. The free rent that had been generously offered by the Pew Charitable Trust didn't hurt either.

Satha and Tom had also made plans to launch the nutritional supplement business together. Shortly before Tom had agreed to become co-owner of the

Bedford property and her business partner, Satha had told Tom that she had resigned from her professorship at Columbia. She said that the university was too devoted to pursuing the study of Western medicine, resulting in reduced opportunities for her to do out-of-the-box research. Only later would it occur to Tom how odd her complaint was since Dr. Mehmet Oz, the physician and complementary medicine advocate whom she falsely claimed was her mentor, had been listed as a Professor of Surgery at Columbia's College of Physicians and Surgeons since 2001. She also said that Columbia had been surprised and perhaps a bit put out when she'd resigned her professorship in order to concentrate on her work with the supplement.

The revelation had been a surprise to Tom, although not necessarily out of the ordinary. Satha recently had been through a divorce, which meant that in many ways she was starting life over. In addition, she had an exciting new prospect on the horizon in the form of a supplement business that Tom truly believed had potential. Besides, the lack of academic demands meant that Satha could devote more time to the day-to-day business operations. Despite the fact that Satha had severed her ties with Columbia, Tom was still willing to embark on this project with her. So he forged ahead full steam. Tom would serve as Chairman of the Board and legal advisor, while Satha would retain her primary role as clinician, researcher, and supplement formulator.

Satha had also put together a Board of Directors that she had hoped she could turn to for advice and support as needed. However, it was a very weak and not at all engaged group. Tom had met with a couple of the directors in person and was introduced to the others by phone. Although Tom did not know the members well, he assessed from their bios and from his conversations with them that they would be of limited help. They had, however, indicated similar interest in the findings of Satha's research and held out special hope for the curcumin-based supplement. Tom was hopeful the group would make for a good team, but he was not optimistic. He sensed that, although bright, the directors knew nothing about business and didn't expect to be called on to do very much, if anything, in the way of running the business.

On the other hand, on the day after his arrival in Bedford, Tom plunged into work on behalf of the supplement company. After examining the business plan that Satha had created, Tom quickly discovered that Satha also knew nothing about business or about business writing. Quite frankly, her business plan was a mess. It was riddled with redundant passages and a preponderance of clinical rather than business language. There were also sections that almost seemed nonsensical, as if she had simply lifted them from various studies by cutting and pasting without implementing appropriate revisions to turn the words into business prose. Also, identical language that was found on page after page was not even given attribution. Although the sloppily drafted business plan caught Tom by surprise, he remembered how Satha had called him in as a partner to supplement her own shortcomings. The business plan was certainly a place for Tom to start adding value and expertise.

Tom scrapped the original business plan in its entirety and began writing it from scratch to make it more artfully drafted and businesslike. Where he was uncertain of clinical information, such as the correct spellings of supplement ingredients or explanations of the efficacy of the products in the reduction of chronic inflammation, Tom consulted Satha. Before too long, he had crafted a succinct business plan that he felt he could comfortably share with his valued contacts in the coming months when he and Satha would be seeking investment dollars to grow the company.

Next, Tom dove into coming up with names for the business and the supplement line itself. A brainstorm of ideas led Tom and Satha to the aforementioned business name of Quintessence of Life, with the product line being called JIVA. Tom liked JIVA for a couple of reasons. In Ayurvedic, *jiva* means "Quintessence of Life," which seemed altogether appropriate for a supplement that could potentially extend people's life spans. In addition, JIVA sounded somewhat like the word *java*. Tom anticipated that this word association might pay off in helping a coffee-loving American public to relate to the supplement line.

Although Tom was neither a technical wizard, nor a professional in visual aesthetics, he enjoyed working with a designer to create the label for the supplement as well as an attractive website that would inform consumers about the product's potential benefits and the locations where it could be purchased. In the design process, they added to the label an icon of Mount Kailash, a historic and spiritual mountain in western Tibet that is honored and respected by adherents of a number of religions. As for the product itself, the plan was to start with the curcumin supplement and then possibly expand the line to include other supplements known for their health benefits.

One day not long after Tom's move to Bedford, Satha invited Tom to tour the Long Island facility where her supplements were formulated, packaged, and readied for distribution. During the drive there, Satha explained how the supplement ingredients were ordered from China, transited through San Diego, and then sent to the processing facility. Satha said that she had provided her unique formulation to the facility staff, and they were responsible for combining ingredients in the right proportions and then packaging them in bottles.

During the visit, Tom and Satha took a quick tour of the area where the shipments from San Diego were currently being stored and then were escorted to an office. The site director, a sturdy-looking, dark-haired Indian man perhaps in his fifties, explained that $3,000 was owed to his company for the shipping costs from San Diego to New York.

"I don't have $3,000," Satha replied, which caught both Tom and the site director off guard. Each had assumed that a professional such as Satha would have a financial plan in place for managing the costs of her inventory. This was the first time that Tom had heard of money being owed for the product, and although it was off-putting that Satha would order a shipment without the funds to cover the costs, Tom knew that the business could not be successful without product. He decided to step up and make the $3,000 payment himself by way of a loan to the company.

Tom had not intended to make any loans to the company, but he was in it now and he would do whatever it took to help it succeed.

Chapter 11

As the weeks unfolded and winter turned into spring and then spring turned into summer, Tom and Satha lived amicably together in the Bedford home. The house was so large that the two of them could live quite independently in their own separate wings, only to meet on the basement level during working hours or perhaps in the kitchen for a meal. However, given the potential for a man and a woman living in such close proximity to enter into a more intimate relationship, Tom had made it clear to Satha from the start that if he moved into the house, it would be as a co-tenant and business partner, not as a lover. He was not physically attracted to Satha. He also knew better than to mix business with that kind of pleasure. Nevertheless, he soon discovered Satha had hoped that the relationship would develop into something more personal.

One night fairly early on, Satha came to Tom's room. It was just after one o'clock in the morning. Tom was lying in bed in a deep sleep when he felt someone warm slip under the covers. It took some moments for Tom to fully awaken. As he became more alert, he could feel the sensation of heat spreading all over his body. A woman had nestled down near his groin and was touching him, rubbing her hands in small circles. Her hands moved across his boxer shorts, up his torso, and to his bare chest. He could feel his nipples harden under her touch, and by the time Tom realized who was in the bed with him, Satha had begun nuzzling her nose into the opening in his boxer shorts. Tom hardened and came to attention in spite of himself. He groaned softly as Satha took him inside her mouth. He could feel her coming down on him, slowly at first and then faster and faster. With each stroke of her moist, taut mouth, Tom lost himself more deeply, as if retreating into the sleep from which he had just awakened.

In this dreamlike state, Tom and Satha rocked in motion together for nearly twenty minutes. Satha sucked and stroked as Tom's back arched and his bottom flexed, giving in to her more and more until he ejaculated in an ecstatic spasm that felt electric.

When it was all done, Satha fell into Tom's arms awkwardly, as she was quite a heavy woman and Tom was thinner than she was. Although they did not stay locked in an embrace, Tom and Satha spent the rest of the night in bed together, sleeping. When Tom awoke, he showered, brushed his teeth, and dressed as usual. Then, before he left the room, he pulled a blanket over Satha so that she would stay warm and covered.

Later that morning, in the kitchen, as Tom made lunch and Satha poured her coffee, Tom decided to address what had happened the night before. "You were kind to visit my room last night, Satha," he said. "And being a man, I must admit that what we did felt good. But you know I am not romantically interested, and it's important to me that we keep our relationship on a professional level for the sake of the business."

Satha responded with a small, coy grin. Tom thought the gesture was condescending in its certainty and seemed to say that she knew that Tom was only going through the motions of drawing boundaries with her for reasons of propriety. That annoying smile widened as Satha said, "We'll see about all of that."

"Satha, I am quite serious," Tom added. "Last night was very pleasurable to be sure, but as I've said before even if the business was not part of the equation, I am not interested in having a romantic relationship with you."

It seemed cold to say that so directly, and yet Tom felt it was necessary in order to be clear. He did not want to lead Satha on. He also did not want to compromise the business's potential, which he had come to believe in fervently with his heart, his mind, and his pocketbook. Yes, Tom had been weak in letting Satha come to him the night before, but now that it was daylight he made it clear that this should not happen again.

From the look on Satha's face, Tom could tell that she finally realized he was serious and that she did not like his rebuff. "Okay, then," she replied politely, reverting to the clinical and professional demeanor she'd presented to Tom at the beginning of their relationship. What Tom didn't realize was that Satha had already decided that she would indeed visit him in his room again at some point in the future, as she was not one to be turned down for anything.

In the meantime, during the early months of their time together, Tom and Satha spent a fair amount of time traveling the country, pitching the supplement's potential to venture capitalists and angel investors with whom Tom was familiar, and urging them to grab a piece of equity in Quintessence of Life early on. These investors were typically Tom's friends, acquaintances, and contacts. Tom, indeed, had numerous heavy-hitting connections, including individuals who had developed successful product lines for Nature's Valley, Odwalla, and the Aveeno brands, among others. With regard to potential overseas investors, Satha said she had a major connection whom she identified as the "soy king" of Singapore. There was also a company in India that she only knew by name but with which she thought they could get a meeting. At this point, however, they were mainly focused on finding investors in the United States, so Tom and Satha traveled to New York City and throughout the tri-state area as well as to Los Angeles, Santa Barbara, Portland, Houston, and the greater Miami area.

Yet, in spite of the warm and friendly relationships that Tom had with many of the potential investors (including some from the Silicon Valley area near San Francisco), their interests did not generally lie in the area of the natural products market. Also, although Satha would present her research findings in an intelligent and compelling way, each visit failed to produce actual funding. The common refrain was that investors might be interested further down the line once the company had demonstrated some traction in the marketplace. After all, they were businessmen and women who were accustomed to hearing good pitches. At the end of the day, however, their interest was simply the bottom line.

With each "no" that Satha and Tom received, Satha grew angrier and angrier. The very same inexperience that had led her to create such a weak business plan early on caused her to carry absurd expectations into these investor meetings as well. Rather than seeing them as positive relationship-building efforts for the future, she saw them as total failures. And when it came to amassing funds to support her vision for the business and her lifestyle, failure was intolerable.

On a drive home from one particular investment meeting in Baltimore, Satha blurted, "Just get us $2 million, Tom. You know rich people and they like you. Just do it."

Tom tried not to take offense at Satha's curt tone and the way in which she seemed to be objectifying his friends. "Satha," he replied as calmly as he could, "Rich people don't get rich just by giving away $2 million. I don't care how wonderful and close they are by way of friendship."

"But we have an incredible product," Satha countered. "Just look at all the research. That should be demonstration enough."

Tom knew that there was a big difference between scientific findings and consumer response to a product, but Satha, whether due to ignorance or greed, simply could not see it.

"I mean, look at Vitawater," she continued. "It said in the *Wall Street Journal* that they received $4 million in funding after just one year and it's just water! Quintessence of Life has real, proven supplements. We should be able to attract even more funding!"

"But Vitawater had a track record. We don't!" Tom replied. "They were already publicly traded, we aren't. They had profits, we don't. You've simply got to stop dreaming. This is business, and we have nothing to show at this time other than a well-drafted business plan and a pretty good website. Get real.

"And even if we were able to garner that kind of investment," Tom continued, "you are going to have to give up a lot more equity in the company than you're ready to do."

"What's wrong with giving investors 2 percent?" she asked. It was an argument that she and Tom had had several times by now. "Given how successful the supplement is going to be, that 2 percent will be lucrative."

Tom could reign in his self-control no longer. "Satha, you've got to be smoking ganja to think that an investor will give us millions of dollars for a mere 2 percent interest in the company. That's not the way these things work! If we are fortunate to find a major investor, be prepared to relinquish working control. That's a given and if you can't accept that, we might as well throw in the towel." Satha remained quiet for a moment as she searched for what to say next, but she couldn't come up with a counter-argument.

When the two of them returned from this particular investor meeting, it seemed as if things with Satha and the business had begun to spiral downward. It was hard to keep it all going. But Tom had never shied from work before, so he continued to plod forward with intensity.

The investors wanted to see a track record with consumers before even considering investing in the supplement. Tom and Satha decided to see if they could establish that track record by showcasing the product at various nutraceutical conventions and expos. The events would give them a chance to put product samples in the hands of consumers, wholesalers, and even potential investors. The end result would be, they hoped, a quantifiable increase in demand and renewed interest among the venture capitalists and investors they'd previously pitched. In addition, they could wander the trade show floor to get the latest information on what was happening in the industry, assess the competition, and make some inroads with potential partners. Success at the expos held out hope that they could finally find the funding they needed, which helped keep Tom's growing frustration at bay.

Although much of his time was dedicated to Quintessence of Life, Tom also had to attend to work for his global nonprofit. In fact, after he had to fire the organization's executive director, Tom had ended up stepping in to fill the role himself while the search committee sought a replacement. In addition, Tom's humanitarian efforts required him to travel internationally. He was also writing a book. As a result, Tom was working fourteen to sixteen-hour days. Yes, Tom had a habit of maintaining a healthy diet and exercising regularly. He was also energized by the sense of purpose behind all of his business and professional activities. Nevertheless, if Tom hadn't had years of experience in operating at this speed, he would have been exhausted by the project and the responsibilities on his plate.

While it was true that Satha had crisscrossed the country with Tom and had presented well at meetings with potential investors, wholesalers, and consumers, when they came back to the home office, Satha turned into a slug. She spent several hours a day sleeping. Sometimes she slept until noon. When she was awake, Tom never saw her do anything that seemed to be productive, and she appeared to lack any motivation at all. Yes, occasionally, she would sit at her computer, but it looked as though she was Internet surfing more than anything else. Tom never saw her doing research of her own. The resignation from her Columbia professorship had left her work day exceedingly empty, so she should have had even more time to do research. Yet she seemed to simply be reading online about research being done by others, especially Dr. Aggarwal. It was frustrating that she showed no inclination to work on Quintessence of Life when they weren't traveling. She simply filled her time by watching TV or sleeping.

When she awoke, she would take piles and piles of pills. She commonly took over fifty pills and capsules a day. Some of them were prescription psychiatric medicines, Tom learned. Most, however, were supplements and vitamins. Tom worried about the contra-indications of Satha taking such a quantity of pills. More than once, Tom had asked her if she was fully aware of the interactive effects of taking so many pills and supplements together. It wasn't his business what she consumed, of course, but he did care about her commitment to the company and, of course, to her health. Satha waved him off with little concern. She always said that she had read about each of them and they all must be good. Admittedly, that had not been the answer he'd expected from a woman who had worked as a Columbia University professor, and it had left him uneasy.

Also worrying was the loss of Naar's excellent assistant, Lisa Yang. Tom had no idea what to make of the new assistant who had replaced Lisa and who now sat in the basement watching TV most of the day as well. This was not to say that Satha and the new assistant were in front of the same television. Satha remained stowed away in the living room upstairs while the poor assistant, unsure of how to spend her time without Satha's direction, twiddled her thumbs, surfed the Internet, or sat in front of the downstairs TV. She did not last long. Satha's assistants generally only lasted about a month at a time, as Satha would vacillate between completely ignoring them or yelling at them to the point where they would quit. Satha would then replace them, one after another. Tom could only look on in amazement as this cycle played itself out more than ten times. Lisa was quite talented and had been stalwart, but she was gone and was starting her own acupuncture business.

Any one of these instances gave Tom some cause to worry about both the business and the state of Satha's mental stability. The incident that nearly pushed him beyond the brink, however, was the day he learned about the change of their business website. They had retained a website designer based in Burlington, Vermont, who had created a very professional and in-depth website replete with links to countless research papers documenting the efficacy of the supplement ingredients. Tom discovered that Satha had pulled this website down and had it replaced with what he could only describe as a rather Mickey Mouse version.

"What in the hell?" Tom asked Satha upon discovering this change. "What happened to the website?"

"I didn't think it was very good," Satha replied, "so I had it taken down and replaced."

Tom knew the outfit that had created the new site. They were nice people. However, their design looked infantile compared to what the Burlington designer had created at great expense.

Tom nearly blew his top. He wanted to scream at Satha, but he knew screaming at her would be neither professional nor productive. Instead, he decided to go for a walk outside with Hercules. Fresh air had always done them both good. But he could not leave the room before telling Satha, "I don't know what you are up to, Satha. But it makes no sense at all."

Chapter 12

The next time Tom spoke to Satha was three weeks before an Anaheim, California, exposition they were going to attend. They would be exhibiting the company and the supplement; the to-do list to get ready for the show was long and, as always, Tom was expected to pay for everything. They needed people to help work the booth. They needed signage and an exhibit display. They needed to ship product and make travel arrangements. Tom had already sent reams of paperwork to the conference planners. He'd reserved the booth and ordered an electricity supply as well as badge scanners and an Internet connection. He'd also gotten the company name on a tote bag giveaway. In addition to the time he had spent planning for the conference, Tom had also laid out what was turning into tens of thousands of dollars. These trade shows cost bundles due to the need to rent space in a good location on the exhibit floor, purchase add-ons, hire help, and lay out funds for flights, meals, and the hotel stay.

Tom had never intended to be a cash cow for the business. Once he committed to something he believed in, however, he would do everything within his power to make it successful. As a result, he kept making loans to the company as they were needed, including for this conference and for the website that Satha had unilaterally canned.

Satha had maintained that she had no funds to contribute to the business, but Tom was starting to doubt this. He'd seen her wire large chunks of money from Singapore to the United States when she had gotten into a financial dilemma that she could not wiggle her way out of. He also knew that Satha had received a home equity loan of $1,495,000 from a National Bank not long before he'd come on the scene. And yet none of this money was ever applied to Quintessence of Life. Seemingly, Satha had stashed it in Singapore, which had by this time become the world's largest tax haven. So he was understandably irritated when Satha continued to maintain that she had no cash to contribute.

Tom stood in the doorway of the second-floor living room, watching as Satha sat on the couch watching television. She sat curled up with a blanket, watching yet another crime investigation show and eating yogurt. A large cupful of pills and capsules was on her right, along with a half-empty bottle of vitamin water.

He called out to Satha, who raised her chin in acknowledgment as she swallowed another spoonful of yogurt. The sight of Satha luxuriating on her couch as she savored a morning snack after Tom had been working on the business since six o'clock in the morning annoyed him. He looked away in irritation. On the TV screen, he saw a tall, brunette female detective standing over a dead body and speaking into her cell phone. The scene then switched to a courtroom, and there was a young twenty-something woman standing before a Judge. The look on her face said she was pleading for something.

"Are these things on nonstop morning through evening?" Tom asked.

"Oh yeah," Satha answered. "You can watch them twenty-four hours a day."

"Well, haven't you seen all of them by now?" Tom asked.

"Yes, I've seen some of them three or four times," Satha responded with what sounded like a note of pride in her voice.

"Well, what about work?" Tom asked.

"My assistant is getting some things done for me right now," Satha replied. This stupefied Tom, as he had just seen Satha's latest assistant sitting at her desk in the basement watching an Internet talk show.

Tom stepped through the doorway and scanned the room. Upon setting his eyes on the TV remote, he grabbed it and hit the mute button.

"That's not nice," Satha said.

But Tom didn't care. "We have to get ready for the nutraceutical expo and I can't do it all myself," he said. "There are decisions to be made. We have things to do. You know, I'm tired of financing this company without you putting in any effort," Tom said. "I've simply become your personal line of credit, it seems. This can't go on forever."

"What do you mean?" Satha asked innocently. "I've been traveling everywhere with you over the past several months."

"Yes, you've been traveling with me, but it's all been on my dime, and everything I have, I've worked and saved for."

As always, Satha had no satisfactory answer to that.

Sighing with resignation at the realization that the issue wouldn't be resolved that day, he let Satha get away with that for the moment and moved on to the next important matter: his visit to India. He was scheduled to travel to India soon to initiate his nonprofit's first Indian site.

"I think I should come with you to India," Satha suggested. "I have an excellent relationship with the soy king in Singapore and we could have a really productive meeting with his people there after leaving India. Moreover, I have relatives in India and they tell me they can put us in touch with important people there as well."

Tom thought about the possibility of having Satha join him. He had to admit that it was actually a realistic suggestion, given her ethnicity. Although he wasn't travelling to India for Quintessence of Life, it seemed like a good opportunity to make connections that might enhance the product line and the ingredients used in it. They were starting with a single product and formulation, but they planned to expand over time. The quality of the ingredients could only be enhanced by staying current and having access to leaders in the industries that cultivated and manufactured their product's components. Also, establishing direct relationships with them might also eventually lead to lower costs.

"I suppose that could work," Tom replied. "We'd have to make your arrangements quickly, though, as my trip is only a short time away."

"Let's do it," Satha continued. "I could also use that time to research some of the exotic plants in different parts of the country."

Tom knew by now that he would be the one financing the trip, and while this did niggle at him, he felt it was worth getting Satha overseas to see some of her contacts in the event that it might open up new business possibilities and opportunities for Quintessence of Life.

So he buried his anger and frustration and left the room to begin preparations for their journey.

Chapter 13

For the India trip, Tom was slated to fly to New Delhi, stay the night, then fly out to Kolkata (formerly Calcutta). From there, he was scheduled to get a car to drive to the West Bengal village of Kalgon. Kalgon, in the Sunderbans area on the Bay of Bengal was arguably in one of the poorest parts of India, so Tom knew he would be inaccessible by phone or Internet for the entire length of his visit once he arrived there.

That first night in India, Tom and Satha decided to dine together. However, Satha got sick after their meal and Tom had to help her back to the room. There Satha situated herself in the bathroom with the door just the slightest bit ajar while she hovered over the toilet and vomited repeatedly. Tom asked Satha if he could help her with anything. When she said no, he undressed and got under the covers to see if he could fall asleep. However, he could hear Satha wretch violently for nearly ten minutes, and, when it did not stop, Tom felt compelled to check on her and make sure that everything was okay. He knocked gently on the bathroom door and when Satha did not answer, Tom nudged it open with his hand.

"Satha?" he asked quietly.

She moved her head one quarter turn in his direction and tried to muster a smile. "Just a little traveler's sickness," Satha said. "My God, that curried sauce seems to be burning a hole in my stomach, and it's made my uterine fibroid bleeding more severe than ever." Satha did have a uterine fibroid problem. It was a longstanding issue and one she frequently complained about.

"Is there anything I can do to help you?" Tom asked

"A cold compress would be nice," Satha replied. "I'm sweating like a dog."

"Sure," Tom said, and he padded over to the towel rack to collect a washcloth. He ran under cold water, which in India, is not very cold. He squeezed out the excess and then walked back toward Satha.

She pulled her long black hair aside to expose her neck, and Tom placed the cold compress on it.

"How does that feel?" he asked.

"I'm a mess," Satha said, "but this helps. Thank you."

"Just call me if you need anything else," said Tom. "I'll be in bed."

Tom awoke two hours later with Satha lying next to him.

"I hope you don't mind if I lay here with you," she said. "I'm sure I'll be fine, but I don't want to be alone in the other bed right now after all that sickness. I feel weak."

"Fine, fine," Tom said. It seemed mean to send her away from him while she was feeling so ill. So Tom and Satha slept side by side for the next few hours.

Eventually, the sky outside their window changed from dark blue to gray as the day began to break. The few hours' sleep seemed to restore Satha to almost normal. Tom, floating in the haze between sleep and wakefulness, could feel her hand reach out toward Tom's groin to feel it. It was hard with the dawn of morning, and that lured her on to touch it further. Satha slipped her hand between Tom's legs and rubbed her hand up and over his erection. Tom awoke and lay there experiencing the sensation of gentle friction without saying anything. One part of him told him he should scoot back and slip out of bed toward the bathroom and a morning shower. The other part urged him to lean in closer to Satha. He only had a moment to escape because if he waited too long, he might drown in the feeling and succumb to it.

But before Tom could act, Satha's head disappeared under the covers, and Tom felt the friction of her hand turn into a cascade of slippery warmth as Satha put her mouth around him as she had done once before in Bedford. She applied firm pressure with her lips that penetrated the top few layers of Tom's skin and stimulated it. "My God, this feels good," thought Tom as he released himself into the warmth. He knew he should pull himself away, but it felt hard to do, like trying to separate industrial strength magnets.

"What the hell?" Tom thought and justified his actions with the rationalization that the two of them were overseas and it was okay to break the routine. It would be different when they went back home again.

Tom let out a slow groan as Satha went up and down over his penis with her mouth until she felt she had drawn Tom to the tense moment before climax. Then, she stopped. She slipped off her underwear and straddled him. As she did so, she tried to ease herself

117

on top of Tom's body in a way that would fit the two of them together, but she could not guide Tom into her opening. She tried again and then again, with Tom's hardness each time poking into her skin, unable to find the place of penetration.

"It's too far back," Satha finally admitted, referring to her unusual anatomy. Because of her rather huge belly, her vaginal opening was set so far back toward where a woman's bottom would normally be it was next to impossible to access from this angle. When she was with a man, he would typically have to penetrate her from behind, but she never gave up hope that she would find the one man who could come at her from the front and make love in the way most other women could experience it.

"You could come in from behind," Satha offered.

Tom imagined the feeling of sliding himself into the juicy tightness of a woman—even this heavyset woman whom he did not love—and decided to give it a try. He rose from the bed and moved to its foot so Satha could position herself on all fours. Tom did nearly the same behind her and then proceeded to successfully enter her. Her wetness closed around him and he let himself go for several seconds until Satha began to let out a series of loud grunts that broke Tom's reverie. With each grunt that Satha released, in rhythm with Tom's thrusts into her, Tom's interest in penetrating Satha lessened. He had lost respect for her, not because of the way they were now having sex with her grunting but because of who he was discovering her to be.

Stingy, ungenerous, lazy.

Tom had once admired Satha for her alleged research work and been drawn to her seemingly spiritual nature (whenever she travelled, she brought a pair of slippers she had purchased from an alleged Indian guru who turned out to be the leader of a cult to which Satha belonged). Now all he could think of was the image of her sitting on the couch back home watching crime shows, eating yogurt, and complaining about why potential investors didn't want to fork over millions of dollars for 2 percent equity in the company.

Tom retreated from the position at the foot of the bed and plopped down with his head back on his pillow. "What's wrong?" Satha asked, and Tom stayed quiet, thinking about how he could explain to her what was going on.

"I should not have done that," Tom said. "You know how I feel about us having a relationship."

"Lighten up," Satha said, and shimmied herself until she was once again astride Tom and had the covers pulled up over her. Down she went on Tom four or five more times, trying to get him to reawaken.

But the moment was ruined. Over the many months they had lived together at the Bedford property, Tom had seen her as she was, and there was no going back.

The following day, Tom took Satha to the Khosla Medical Institute in Gurgaon, where she'd be getting Panchakarma treatments at a respected Ayurvedic healing center, which is associated with Transcendental Meditation. Satha had serious health problems involving uterine fibroids, which apparently had been a medical problem for much of her adult life. Her fibroids caused her to bleed profusely at times and not all that infrequently. The condition could be life threatening if not treated properly, so Tom did not begrudge her desire to fit in some unique healing work on this trip along with their business tasks. He only hoped that she would follow through on her promise to meet with the soy king and investigate new ingredients for their supplement line without getting stuck on just her personal agenda.

Tom left Satha in the safe hands of the Ayurvedic doctors at the Ayurvedic center and then plunged headlong into his work for his nonprofit. Having already met in New Delhi with the local Board of Trustees for the Indian branch of the nonprofit, he then traveled, as mentioned, to the remote village of Kalgon in the Sunderbans area of West Bengal, India. While there, Tom made an executive decision that the organization's first site in India would not be in the vicinity of the Taj Mahal and Jaipur in Rajasthan but, rather, in one of the poorest villages in one of the poorest regions of India. He was simply that impressed by the people of Kalgon Gram and with an inspirational leader in the village, a man who truly walked in the shoes of Gandhi. Tom and the village leader were to become the best of friends and remain so today.

After two weeks of work in the village, Tom returned to New Delhi to reconnect with Satha. They initially were to travel on to Singapore. However, when Tom returned to New Delhi, not far from Gurgaon, he called and spoke to Satha, who was still at the Khosla Medical Institute. Satha informed him that she couldn't enter Singapore, the country of her citizenship, nor could the soy king meet them in India. She refused to provide an explanation for why she wasn't allowed to enter Singapore other than a muddled answer about the influence her ex-husband had with the government.

So Tom traveled by taxi to Gurgaon and walked into the Khosla Medical Institute, where he was scheduled to reconnect in person with Satha. A nurse standing behind the receptionist desk immediately dropped her paperwork when she heard Tom ask for Satha.

"Did you say you're here to see Satha Naar?" the nurse asked.

"Yes, I am," Tom said.

"Sir, you have got to get your friend back to the United States immediately. She's been bleeding profusely since she arrived and she needs treatment— a major Western operation that we can't give her. We don't have either the necessary equipment or the training."

Tom squinted his eyes in puzzlement, trying to make sense of what was going on.

"We had no way of reaching you while you were gone," the nurse continued. "The doctors will be so glad to see that you're back. They've just been trying to keep her alive until you returned."

It was not long before Tom learned the full story of what had happened while he was gone. On her very first day of treatment at the Ayurvedic center, the Panchakarma treatment triggered a terrible reaction in Satha that brought on the most exaggerated bleeding of her fibroids ever. The fibroids had been bleeding profusely ever since, and the medical institute was doing all it could to stem the effects and keep Satha alive. Tom had to get Satha back to the United States for proper treatment. Panchakarma, a fine Ayurvedic treatment for most maladies, turned out to be the worst of hells for Satha's fibroid problem.

Worried for Satha, Tom moved into action quickly. They were able to get her on a flight home and on the calendar of a surgeon in the Northern Westchester Hospital in Mount Kisco who could help her. As luck would have it, the best expert in the tri-state area regarding Satha's condition was employed at that hospital. He performed the procedure that probably saved Satha's life. It was major surgery, which stopped the bleeding by basically cauterizing all of the capillaries that fed into the uterus. A few days later, Satha was sent home with Tom. As she was bedridden, Tom took care of her until she was well again. He couldn't fail to notice, however, that Satha's three adult children, who lived within an easy driving distance of the hospital, did not come for even a single visit. In fact, they didn't even call to see how she was doing.

Chapter 14

A few months later, Tom sat in his home office, opening the mail, and found a letter addressed to Satha from Columbia University. As the Chairman of the Board of Quintessence of Life, Tom was copied on the letter, which read as follows:

Dear Ms. Naar:

It has been brought to our attention that you have misrepresented yourself as a former member of Columbia University's Mailman School of Public Health. You have never held a position here. Desist immediately from this misrepresentation, or the University will take whatever steps it deems necessary and appropriate.

The letter was signed by the general counsel of Columbia University.

As Tom read those words, a great ringing in his ears began as the walls of his office started to close in on him. He wanted to run to the toilet and vomit, but it felt as if his legs were glued to his chair. What had he just read? Was it possible that Satha had never been employed by Columbia? The university masthead on the letter looked authentic, and Tom could not think of any reason why he should believe the letter was not real. But if what it said was true, the very foundation of his relationship with Satha was a complete sham.

Tom had an instant flashback to the day he first met Satha, who had been wearing a white lab coat and a stethoscope, on Columbia's campus. She had said they could meet on the quad, as it easy to find, but Tom now wondered why she hadn't met him closer to the Mailman campus, twenty blocks away. And why had she never offered to give him a tour of her lab or her office?

Other questions arose in his mind. Why hadn't her adult children visited her when she'd been seriously ill? How could she not have had a relatively paltry $3,000 to pay the Long Island facility when Tom knew she had been able to wire large sums of money to the tax haven of Singapore? How could she complain about an overemphasis on Western medicine at Columbia when her so-called mentor, Dr. Oz, a champion of complementary medicine, had been on the staff since 2001? Did she actually even know him at all?

Tom grappled with the frightening idea that Satha was not who she said she was—that he had moved across the country for, and by this time had poured hundreds of thousands of dollars into a business whose majority owner suddenly stood revealed as a con artist.

Determined to confront Satha, Tom tucked the letter under his arm and went looking for her. It was no surprise, really, that Tom found her on the second floor watching one of her ridiculous crime shows as she crunched her way through a bag of potato chips.

Tom walked directly into the room, found the remote, and turned off the TV. He stood in front of the black screen and looked directly at Satha. Startled by Tom's uncharacteristic aggression, Satha gaped at him as she pulled the open bag of potato chips a little closer to her.

Tom held the letter before her. "Did you or did you not work in a teaching capacity or in any capacity at Columbia University?" he demanded.

"Yes, I did, Tom. You know I did," she replied.

"Then why do I have a letter here from the university itself saying that you were never employed by them?"

Satha stuttered a moment but eventually stammered out an explanation. "Well, the university never formally hired me, but my friend allowed me to do research there," she said.

Tom wasn't buying it. "What the fuck does that mean? What friend? What research did you actually do? Is your life just a made up lie?" "Fool me once, shame on you; fool me twice, shame on me," he thought. "You've been lying to me, Satha. You've been lying to the whole world. All along. What are you? Are you an absolute fraud?"

"Of course not," Satha insisted as her voice jumped an octave. "You've seen the details of my research. You've seen the supplements. Look at our business plan. Look at the stacks of boxes in the garage. How much more real can this all be?"

Tom still wasn't buying it. It was as if he and Satha had been living in a world made only of knitting yarn and someone had pulled the string that unraveled

125

it. Tom thought of everything that had passed between him and Satha over the past two and a half years. How much of it was false and how much, if any, was true he wondered?

Was she even a doctor of any sort? She had always presented herself as a medical professional with vast training in and knowledge of oncology, cardiology, and neurology, having been mentored for ten years by Dr. Mehmet Oz. Was any of this true? Had she conducted any of her own research, or was it just one big Internet-based cut–and-paste job? Tom remembered how stilted and redundant her writing had appeared in the original business plan she had presented to him. Had Satha actually formulated the supplements they were now selling, as she had represented, or was she just peddling someone else's product? Could the supplement really help people or was the last twenty-four months of Tom's work to bring it to market a total waste? Tom felt more and more nauseated by the minute.

In an effort to dispel his queasiness, Tom lobbed question after question at Satha. He was not surprised that she found a way to backpedal into and out of every answer. As much as he wanted to drill Satha down to the bone to uncover the truth, he realized that, if she was indeed a con artist, the conversation would be pointless. He would have to get his answers a different way.

The following day, Tom and Satha found themselves in White Plains, where they had long been scheduled to make a presentation about Quintessence of Life. Satha would be giving a talk to a group of thirty or so people on the topic of reducing chronic inflammation in order to prevent and cure illness. Tom attended only because he had committed prior to yesterday's awful discovery about Satha being a fake, and he did not want to fail to follow through on a promise to a good organization. He did not need to do much at the event other than meet and greet attendees at the beginning and end. So once Satha began to speak, Tom settled into his chair and tried his best to listen even though he now feared that everything that came from Satha's mouth was trash.

Satha began her talk by explaining what chronic inflammation was and then listing some of the health conditions her supposed research linked to inflammation. She went on to describe the ways in which "her" research had shown that curcumin seemed to have a curative effect on chronic inflammation.

Having already heard this information on several occasions, Tom started to tune out Satha's words, but then she stumbled upon a new topic that broke Tom out of his daydream. Tom heard Satha mention "Panchakarma treatments."

"Curcumin is just one of the alternative items available to us to improve our health," Satha said. "One of my recent favorites is Panchakarma, an Ayurvedic treatment that is popular in India for addressing virtually every type of problem. I can testify firsthand to the power of these treatments."

Tom leaned in to listen more closely to what Satha would say next.

"Three months ago, I had a terrible, terrible uterine fibroid problem that I might have died from due to internal bleeding," Satha explained to the group. "But because I underwent Panchakarma treatments, the bleeding ceased and my fibroids were cured."

At that moment, Tom felt as shaken as if an earthquake had struck and lifted the ground several inches while flinging everything off the walls. Satha's latest lie was not just self-serving; it had the potential to be fatal. She had nearly died from the Panchakarma treatments. Did she want others to face the same fate? What spurred her to speak such gibberish? Tom and she both knew the truth: Surgery—Western medicine—had healed her!

Tom immediately began thinking of liability. Here a supposed professor of epidemiology, allegedly once on the staff of one of the most prestigious schools in the world, was telling people that what is a fine treatment for most people is also a cure for someone with uterine fibroid problems. He knew the reverse to be true, and he prayed that none of the women in the room had a uterine fibroid problem.

Satha's lie had told Tom everything he needed to know. She was a one-hundred-percent, absolute, unadulterated bullshit artist. And he had fallen for her act lock, stock, and barrel—just as others had apparently done for much of her life.

Did he ever feel like a fool!

Tom scanned his mind and thought of the countless others who had fallen for Satha's scam, too. He remembered how Dr. Venkat Aggarwal, the highly educated and esteemed medical scientist at the MD Anderson Cancer Center in Houston had told Tom that Satha's research may have, in fact, been more advanced than that of his own team. This was after Dr. Aggarwal had spoken to Satha several times on the phone. Tom thought of each member on the Quintessence of Life board of directors whom Satha had convinced to lend his or her name to the cause. And Tom thought of the people who listened to Satha speak on an online talk program to which Tom had introduced Satha. Was it likely that they also believed whatever came out of the mouth of this "noted professor" of Columbia University? Tom had been deceived, but so had all of these other reputable individuals. In spite of her many flaws, Satha could speak intelligently on the topics she claimed were her areas of study. She presented very well in professional settings. Now Tom realized that she had just been parroting the research of others, such as Dr. Aggarwal's team, back at him and the public. And she clearly didn't mind throwing in fabrications when useful, such as the one about the Panchakarma treatments. She seemed to prey on people's desire for hope and healing. Tom thought back to that day when he first met Satha in search of a cure for his dying brother, and it made him feel ill.

Tom did not know if Quintessence of Life was over as a company or whether the supplement actually had the capacity to alleviate serious health conditions. He planned to think these things through to find answers. What he did know, without a single doubt, was that his relationship with Satha—housemate, business partner, and occasional seductress—was over for good.

Chapter 15

Three days later, Tom was sitting in his home office thinking about the upcoming meeting he had scheduled for Satha and himself with PepsiCo to see if the international food products and beverage company would be interested in investing in the product line. Tom bridled at the thought of continuing to engage with Satha as a business partner, and yet this meeting with PepsiCo was huge. Tom had leveraged a major contact there, Dr. Rashid Lan. Dr. Lan was PepsiCo's chief scientific officer and, in effect, the number three person in the entire Pepsi chain of command. He was orchestrating a session for us to meet with a group of top-level Pepsi officers. Dr. Lan had more than fifty thousand employees underneath his leadership, so to get such a meeting for Quintessence of Life was an incredible opportunity and Tom still believed in the efficacious properties of JIVA even though he now knew that Satha had nothing to do with its development. If he and Satha could present persuasively enough at the meeting with the PepsiCo team, Quintessence of Life might still have a chance to go from no-name to big-name in a matter of months.

It's not that Tom cared about financial riches, as he already had enough in the bank to ensure his retirement. Money had simply never been the driving force in his life. He certainly didn't want to be destitute, and it was important to him that he have the financial freedom to travel and seek out new experiences. But, most of all, Tom's desire was to help those in the world who lacked opportunities that those in North America and Western Europe have historically enjoyed since the advent of the Industrial Revolution. He especially strove to promote literacy, and his desire to also promote health and reduce disease was well-known. As a result, any financial gain resulting from either a sale to PepsiCo or any part of Quintessence of Life business activities would have the possibility of furthering his humanitarian work.

Nevertheless, Tom did have more mundane financial concerns. Quintessence of Life had never made a profit. In fact, the company had lost money each and every month for the four years in which it had been in existence. The company was only staying afloat thanks to the generosity of Thomas Strahan. At this point, Tom had loaned the company more than $350,000. He'd also paid hundreds of thousands of additional dollars toward several of Satha's other debts. In all, Tom had put more than $600,000 toward attempting to make Quintessence of Life successful, and in keeping the Smith Farm Road property from foreclosure.

Since Tom had learned of Satha's fakery earlier that week, he had done a good deal of reading, researching, and reflecting. He needed to know whether the supplement line truly had the potential to help others as he and Satha had been positing for the past few years. If it didn't, he would immediately pull his support. If it did, he would consider how he could continue promoting the product without remaining intricately linked with Satha, for whom he had lost all respect.

During his research, Tom reached out again to Dr. Aggarwal at the MD Anderson Cancer Center in Houston. He wanted to know what Dr. Aggarwal thought of the supplement's ingredients and whether, on the basis of his own research, he believed they offered value to consumers. Upon learning about Satha's deception, Dr. Aggarwal was shocked and dismayed, and he agreed to offer Tom his opinion on the supplements. It was the least he could do after introducing Tom to a con artist.

Although Dr. Aggarwal did not enter the supplement into his own rigorous research testing, he did assure Tom that the main ingredient, curcumin, had been correlated with many positive health effects in his own research, from reducing the incidence of cancer to alleviating the symptoms of Lyme disease. If Tom could verify the quality of the curcumin, then he could feel comfortable in offering the product for sale to the public as a supplement.

Next, Tom went about learning more about the formulation. He spoke directly to the manufacturing house and discovered that the supplements were not Satha's unique formulation as she had asserted. It was an off-the-shelf product that she was importing to the United States from China and simply having the label Tom had designed placed on the container. Tom, of course, was disturbed to discover yet another one of Satha's lies, but he was no longer surprised. Also, Tom could see that this lie did not mean that the supplement itself was ineffective. In bringing the supplement to the United States and to the marketplace, they were potentially providing a service to consumers who might not otherwise have access to it.

Tom decided to proceed with the PepsiCo meeting in good conscience, especially since now Dr. Lan's reputation was also on the line.. Although he did not want to spend another minute with Satha, he decided to follow through on the meeting to see where it might lead the company. Afterward, they could look for a way to dissolve their partnership. But he wasn't ready to give up on his mission to help others without following through on this one last opportunity.

Unfortunately, his decision to stay until he saw the outcome of the PepsiCo meeting meant that he was still subject to Satha's old tricks. The day before the PepsiCo meeting, Satha showed up in Tom's office to drop another bomb. "I need $20,000 for the PepsiCo presentation," she said. "Will you loan it me?" Her confidence was surprising in the wake of Tom's accusation that she was a fraud.

Tom was signing some paperwork on his desk and nearly ran his pen off the page upon hearing Satha's bold request. "Loan you more money?" he repeated. "I've been doing that now for several years, Satha, but it's obvious that you don't know what a loan is since, from what I now know, you've never repaid one and that's why people keep suing you. Seemingly, you don't pay or repay for much of anything unless someone first sues you."

She actually had the nerve to say, "OK, Tom, but I will repay you. Look, I'll even write you a check right now that you can hold and cash in three weeks when I bring additional money in from Singapore."

Tom initially pushed back at Satha. The last thing he wanted to do was throw more money down the sinkhole of Satha's lies. But he realized that they still had to get through the PepsiCo meeting. Since he did not want to give her any reason to sabotage it, he acquiesced.

"Okay," he said, "but only if you write me that check you were talking about and promise not to screw up the PepsiCo meeting."

Satha just smiled and left. A few minutes later, she returned with a checkbook. She handed Tom a check for $20,000 dated three weeks from then and told him that he could cash it on that date at her bank in Banksville. Tom, in turn, then wrote Satha a check and filed hers with his papers, as he had every intention of depositing it on the date in question. He doubted that the check would clear, but he would certainly give it a try.

When Tom and Satha arrived at the PepsiCo meeting the following day and shook hands with the five representatives present, Tom couldn't help but obsess on how the meeting might go. He had implored Satha multiple times before the meeting to make sure everything in her domain of the presentation was prepared. He didn't want any glitches, as this was their big chance—and no doubt their last one.

As Tom had seen her do many times before, Satha gave her spiel quite effectively. She then took the almond milk that she had brought to the presentation and mixed it with the powdered form of the supplement for tasting by the PepsiCo team. Then it happened.

One of the attendees took a large swallow of the drink—and then nearly spit it across the room! She made it to the trashcan just seconds before spewing. Another attendee flared his nostrils before he began to drink and said, "This smells rancid or something." The woman at the trashcan said, "It tastes awful!" Tom and Satha each grabbed themselves a cup of the mixture to investigate further.

Indeed, the mixture smelled foul, which was not at all typical for the drink. Tom approached the carton of almond milk and took a big sniff through the opening. Sure enough, the almond milk had spoiled. Satha, who had been in charge of purchasing and packing the ingredients, had not even checked it before bringing it to a high-level meeting with top-ranking executives from the world's second largest food and beverage supplier.

Tom glared at Satha. "Do you have another container of almond milk?" he asked her, in the hope that she'd brought a backup.

"Uh, no," Satha said angrily, and it was clear that her anger was aimed at Tom rather than herself.

Mortified, Tom did his best to explain away the gaffe to the PepsiCo team and try to salvage the meeting. "This is really unfortunate, as we've never had this problem before," he said, "but it appears we've gotten a rotten batch of almond milk, which is spoiling the taste of the supplement. Please accept our deepest apologies. This is not at all the way JIVA tastes like when properly mixed. We couldn't be more embarrassed."

The woman by the trashcan had returned to her seat by that time and pulled a small cloth handkerchief from her purse, which she was using to wipe the corners of her mouth. She cleared the milk residue away, but her expression indicated that the sensation of disgust was going to linger.

It was hard to rebound from the putrid taste of the spoiled almond milk. Soon enough, Tom and Satha were packing up their things and shaking hands politely with the PepsiCo group. On the drive back to the home office, Tom could not help but reprimand Satha. His voice wasn't raised, but his tone was filled with derision.

"My God, do you know how hard it was for me to get that meeting? Very few people could have arranged for a meeting at that level with Pepsi. It was our big chance and you just blew it."

"What do you want me to do, Tom?" Satha replied. "How many of those presentations have we done where the milk has always been fine? Just count them."

Tom knew that to some degree the spoiled milk was just bad luck, but he also knew that Satha never seemed to employ the same level of attention to detail that he used to prepare for his part in these presentations or to run the business in general. Had she done so, maybe there would have been a backup carton of almond milk at the PepsiCo meeting.

As soon as he could, Tom made a phone call to his key PepsiCo contact, Dr. Lan, to ask for another opportunity to have the group assess the supplement. He and Satha were indeed given the opportunity, but this time, the tasting and testing would be done by a Pepsi research team in Chicago. Tom was grateful that Dr. Lan, in effect, had given them another opportunity, but the business chance of a lifetime had been lost. Tom and Satha simply packed up some supplement containers and sent them to an address in Chicago as instructed. A few weeks later, Tom received a letter from a Pepsi employee in Chicago saying that the company would not, "after preliminary testing, be doing further research."

Obviously, the reply from PepsiCo was not at all what Tom had hoped for. Even as he saw Satha's image withering before him, he still believed in the product itself and he wanted the professional effort he had invested and the money he had loaned over the past four years to make a positive difference. So Tom made one last attempt to resurrect their PepsiCo opportunity.

Because Tom didn't recognize the name of the person who had signed the letter, he called Dr. Lan to determine if she was in a position to make such a decision. Dr. Lan said that she was not all that high in the chain of command, but that he would not override her decision given the fiasco that had previously occurred at the Westchester County corporate headquarters of PepsiCo. He felt that his own objectivity and credibility would be on the line if he pushed further.

And that was that. Another good business lead—the best one they had ever had—had just drained away from them.

Chapter 16

After the PepsiCo endeavor failed, Tom had had enough. He had become more and more despondent over their business prospects. So he told Satha, that was it. They couldn't keep the business going, not with any more of his money. He told her that he hoped she could continue with the business and wished her success but that he would neither loan nor invest any more money.

As for Satha, after the PepsiCo failure, her behavior had become more and more peculiar. In addition to obsessively watching her crime shows day and night and continuing to take her piles of supplements and medications, she started talking about setting the house on fire. A few times, she talked about doing it in order to get the insurance proceeds. She said that a friend of hers had collected a lot of money by setting fire to his business, or so she claimed. Such comments alarmed Tom as he had once lost a home to a fire. Shortly after that, there was an incident that only increased his fear.

One day at the house when Tom was in the basement talking to a visiting friend about the best way to separate his and Satha's assets, he saw a bizarre scene. Tom's attention, as well as that of his friend, was drawn to the French door that led into Satha's office which was adjacent to the room where Tom exercised and stored most of his files.

"Oh my God, Tom, look," said his friend as he peered through the door's glass panes. He stepped back so Tom could get a better view.

Tom gasped. Multiple lit candles (probably 40 or more) were dotting the floor as Satha's small dog, a untrained white Maltese, ran around them as if they were part of a playful obstacle course. Tom grabbed the door handle and tried to open it so he could extinguish the minefield of candles, but to no avail. The door was locked.

Suddenly, Tom remembered of the occasion a month before when Satha had told him of the friend whose store had burned down and how he had received hundreds of thousands of dollars in insurance proceeds. Then Tom remembered how Satha had regularly double-checked to make sure that he'd paid the homeowners insurance premium. Tom had no doubt that Satha was trying to find another way to get her hands on money. It seemed that there was no end to her willingness to cheat and scam. Apparently, committing arson wouldn't bother her at all if she felt she could get away with it.

As the candles kept burning, Tom wondered what he should do next. He wanted to get Satha down there to resolve the situation, but she had left the house several hours before and he had no idea where she might be. He considered breaking down the door or calling 911. Finally, he grabbed a hammer and shattered a window pane in the French door. Carefully, he reached his hand through to the door knob and turned the lock. He opened the door, stepped carefully over the broken glass, and headed directly toward the candles. In her excitement to see Tom, Satha's dog tripped over a candle and knocked the flame to the floor. Before the candle could make more than a dark spot of soot on the carpet, Tom raced over to it and blew out the flame. He and his friend then extinguished every other candle in the room.

Once the situation was under control, the two of them sat on the back terrace to recount what they had just seen. Although he was not sure yet how to do it, Tom felt that he could not separate himself from Satha fast enough.

To Tom's surprise, that opportunity presented itself within the week. It began with Satha urging Tom to attend one of her psychiatric appointments. "Why on earth would I want to go to one of your psychiatric sessions?" Tom asked, suspicious that Satha was simply trying to get him to cover the bill for her lifestyle once again.

"Because she also works as a facilitator," Satha replied, "and she can help us talk through our differences."

On the one hand, Tom wanted to run away from this invitation as fast as possible. It wasn't as if he and Satha were dissolving a marriage. On the other hand, it might be a way to sort out how to divide the business and the house, which were still shared assets at this point. Yet by this time, knowing that Satha was a pathological liar, he didn't trust anything that Satha asked him to do. It wasn't until she badgered him that Tom finally agreed to attend. What the hell? He probably didn't have anything to lose by giving it a try.

After a series of meetings with Satha's psychiatrist, Satha offered to buy Tom out of his share of the Quintessence of Life business for $300,000, and the psychiatrist–facilitator wrote up a concise agreement in clear English that both Satha and Tom looked at and orally agreed to.

Upon hearing of the agreement between Satha and Tom, the facilitator said, "Why don't you each take this home, review it with your attorneys, and think about it for a while? If you're both still comfortable with it, come back in a week, and the two of you can sign it and I'll sign it as a witness that you have a legally binding agreement."

Was it possible that Satha was actually willing to buy Tom out of the business? Maybe she was willing to pay a price to get rid of him since he now knew about a number of her falsehoods, including that she was not a doctor of epidemiology and was never employed as a professor or in any other capacity at Columbia University. The $300,000 would not even come close to covering the many loans Tom had made to the company for everything from buying products to covering marketing costs, salaries, and travel expenses. But Tom welcomed a clean exit in the form of a cash buyout. He waited to see what would happen at the next appointment with the facilitator.

A few days later and before the next appointment, Satha came to Tom's office and said that after consulting with her attorney, she wanted to amend the agreement. Tom listened skeptically to see what Satha would suggest. "I'd like to amend the agreement to give me an additional two months to make my payment to you," she said. "That gives me more time to bring the money ashore without raising eyebrows."

Tom thought for a moment and tried to assess whether this was an attempt by Satha simply to wiggle out of the agreement. Nevertheless, if she signed the document, she would still be legally bound to pay him for his share of the business, not now but two months from now, which was all the same to him. Tom allowed the amendment, and he and Satha signed the agreement at the next session with the facilitator, who proceeded to sign as a witness.

Back at the home, Tom warned Satha not to play games with the agreement. "I know your history of not paying anyone unless they first sue you. If you don't pay in the promised time frame," he told her, "I will sue you. Believe me, I will."

"No, you won't," Satha countered. "You're too nice to do that."

"Satha," Tom replied, "I can and I will sue you, I promise you."

Satha shrugged her shoulders in a carefree sort of way and looked out the car window without saying another word.

At about the same time, the $20,000 check that Satha gave to Tom for his loan before the PepsiCo meeting came due for depositing. Tom had dutifully waited for the three weeks to pass, and on the date that Satha had told him he could cash it, Tom went to the local bank where they both did business.

Tom stood at the counter as the teller entered the check information into the computer. The teller, whom Tom knew well from his previous dealings with the bank, looked at Tom with a crinkled brow and said, "Sir, I'm sorry, but that particular account has insufficient funds."

Tom rolled his eyes and sighed in disgust. "I'm sorry, it's not your fault," he said. "I've just been dealing with this woman for years now and she has yet to pay me back for a single one of my loans."

"Of course, I understand your frustration," replied the teller. He then looked at the computer screen in front of him a bit more closely and seemed to be scrolling down with his eyes.

"Wait a minute," he said. "There is actually substantial money that recently arrived from Singapore, and you are a signatory on that account. If you'd like, you can withdraw the $20,000 from that second account where there are sufficient funds."

And so that is exactly what Tom did.

Later, when Satha discovered that the withdrawal had gone through, she turned red in the face and started screaming at Tom. Frankly, Tom did not care. It was the only time that Satha had ever "repaid" a single one of his loans to the company, and he felt not the least bit apologetic.

Chapter 17

When the agreed upon time came for Satha to buy Tom out of the business, Tom paid a visit to the part of the house in which she was ensconced.

"Have you brought more of the money you have stashed in Singapore ashore so that you can pay me the $300,000?" Tom asked.

"No," Satha replied casually, as she dusted some crumbs off of her shirt. "I'm not going to pay you."

Tom could feel his heartbeat quicken. "Well, I'm going to have to bring suit against you then, since that seems to be the only thing that motivates you."

"You know," Satha looked at Tom in the eyes apparently taking him more seriously now, "I'll pay you if you start paying for the house, the taxes, and all of the business expenses again."

"No, Satha," Tom replied. "The spigot has been turned off."

Satha sunk a little deeper into the armchair where she was sitting as Tom told her he would be talking to a local attorney, but she didn't respond.

Tom left the room in disgust and returned to his office to pay some bills. At the top of the pile was another foreclosure letter. Tom had been staving off foreclosure on the home for the entire time he had been living there. Although he paid half of the mortgage payment every month, plus taxes and all home-related expenses, Satha had never paid her share—not even once. In fact, she had not been paying anything by way of household expenses. In the beginning and before he had become aware of Satha's criminal activity, Tom had been sympathetic to Satha's circumstances as a divorcee. In fact, he had even gotten Andrew Cuomo's office involved to help hold off foreclosure. Although now New York's Governor, Cuomo was at the time of Tom's request for assistance the State's Attorney General. Cuomo's office had opened a file at Tom's request and started to investigate the foreclosure action that had been brought by the bank from which Satha had received $1,495,000. Tom had also spent countless hours on the phone with the mortgage company and anyone who could help keep the house under its current ownership.

The loan on the house was in Satha's name. One of the incentives Satha had offered in exchange for Tom helping her with the business and helping her to stave off foreclosure was a deed of a tenant-in-common ownership interest in the house. Needless to say, the agreement did not burden Tom with any financial obligations for her mortgage for which she—and she alone—had received close to one and a half million dollars. Although they were to share household expenses, Satha did not do so and Tom, of necessity, ended up paying all of them. Still, it would not do any good for either of them if the house was foreclosed upon.

So Tom did all that he could to forestall foreclosure of the house. He drafted scores of legal documents, retained New York–based counsel, spoke daily with bank representatives, and did continuous research. Had Tom been billing Satha for his services, his fee would have been well over a million dollars. As for Satha, she did not help their case at any time. From what he could gather, after Satha had received the $1.495 million loan, she failed to make more than one or two partial mortgage payments on the house. She did this by using the money she had "borrowed" (i.e., stolen) from the bank. Then she just quit paying altogether and failed to respond to any inquiries from the mortgage company.

A process server for the bank came repeatedly to the home to serve Satha with foreclosure papers, as Tom was initially only able to stave off foreclosure for so long. Satha would pretend each time that she saw the process server that she was simply a visitor at the home and that Ms. Naar was in India. She would then slam the door.

One sunny afternoon, as Tom exited the driveway in his car, he saw the process server throw a manila envelope on the road just beyond the edge of the driveway. Documents went flying out and the server screamed, "As far as I'm concerned, Ms. Naar has been served and my affidavit will so state!" Tom stopped the car and picked up the paperwork that was strewn all about the road. He took the manila folder in his hand and dusted off some dirt and leaves as best he could. There he found the name of the mortgage company in bold letters in the return address, with Satha's name in the main address field. Tom got in his car, which was idling in the driveway and read the documents. All of the foreclosure papers that the process server representing the bank had been trying to serve Satha with over the past few weeks were there. Tom imagined that the process server's anger and desperation had led her to her dramatic abandonment of the papers at the base of the driveway.

What Tom discovered once he dug deeper into the mortgage problem was that Satha had gotten a $1,495,000 mortgage on the house by claiming that she made $33,000 per month at her faux job at Columbia University. Clearly, the bank that loaned her the money had not conducted any due diligence whatever before loaning her almost $1.5 million dollars. In fact, Tom was to learn that the process had been far shadier than that.

Satha had, at one point, come clean with Tom and explained that a broker in Indianapolis whom she had never met told her she was to drive to an address far out on Long Island and that she had to be there at precisely 5:00 p.m. on a certain date. Satha was to bring her completed paperwork showing that she made $33,000/month as a Professor of Epidemiology at Columbia University, as well as a property appraisal in the amount of $3 million that Satha and the broker had made up. She was to do this even though she had no job and thus no income at all and even though she would be making these statements under penalty of perjury – a felony under New York law. If she did this, the broker said Satha would receive $1,495,000 from the bank. However, if she did not arrive at the designated address at precisely the right time, the opportunity would be lost.

According to Satha, after arriving at a small office building at the appointed time, she was met by a nineteen or twenty-year-old woman. The building was not a bank of any kind, and the young woman just pointed to where on the document Satha was to sign.

She then said that Satha would receive a call when the money was to be picked up.

Tom shuddered to think about all of the criminal wrongdoing in which Satha and the broker had engaged in order to obtain such a huge sum of money from WAMU. At first, he found the story impossible to believe, even given the crazy shenanigans going on in the housing industry between 2005 and 2007. But Satha later told the same story to the New York–licensed attorney Tom had retained for her. The attorney told her that she had committed a felony under New York law and could go to prison but for the expiration of the statute of limitations. Had she been convicted, she would no doubt have gone to prison for both bank and real estate fraud and no one would have felt the least bit sorry for her.

Nevertheless, although she might be able to escape criminal punishment, she did still owe the bank on the mortgage. However, Satha—to the best of Tom's understanding anyway—said that she never had any intention of paying the money back. She was hoping that Tom, with his contacts and legal skills, could keep the house out of foreclosure. And to be sure, Tom had pulled all of his strings to stop it until now, but he wasn't sure how much more he could or even wanted to do. He was done letting Satha take advantage of him so she could maintain her desired way of life by stealing money and using him as a personal line of credit.

After Tom filed his complaint against Satha for failing to pay on the promissory note she owed him, Tom's attorney sent her an e-mail with a scanned copy of the complaint. Next, someone came to the house to serve the papers to Satha in person. Upon receiving them, Satha threw the papers down on her office floor and declared, "I already saw them, and I'm moving out anyway!"

It was a look into the way Satha's childish mind worked—as if by moving out, she could solve the problem. As if by leaving the house on Tom's shoulders, she would suddenly become absolved of owing the mortgage or of paying Tom for his share of the business that she had agreed, in writing and in front of a witness, to pay. As if by moving out, she would win rather than Tom.

Nevertheless, Tom was very happy she was moving out. After Tom had quit paying Satha's expenses, Satha had become both verbally and physically abusive with Ashley and with Tom's assistant, Natalie. By this time, Tom realized that not only was Satha a pathological liar, but she might be certifiably insane. As such, he was especially worried about the physical well-being of his daughter, of his assistant, and of his dog as well.

Satha did move out that very day; she took whatever things she could carry in her SUV and drove away. Tom did not see her again for approximately ten days, when she returned unexpectedly, indicating that she was back to gather more of her belongings. "Fair enough," Tom thought. Although he had no interest in seeing Satha, it was only reasonable that she be able to clear out whatever of her things she wished to have.

Tom did not follow Satha around the house as she gathered her things but, rather, continued to work in his office. Consequently, Tom did not see what she took, given that Satha had her own office and separate wing of the house. However, Tom assumed she was gathering papers, clothing items, and other such possessions, which was fine with him. In fact, he wondered if he could pass the time without having to speak with her at all.

Near the end of her visit, Satha answered that question by appearing in Tom's office, her eyes squinted in anger and her nostrils flaring. Satha banged her hand against the wall in three loud slaps as she yelled deeply, "I am going to get you, and I know just how to do it!" Then she left.

What Tom did not notice is that among the items she took with her were the keys to Tom's car, his truck, and his large camper that was also parked on the property.

Had Tom seen what she'd done and stopped her before she could abscond with the keys, he might have prevented the legal ordeal that followed, a Satha-generated nightmare that threatened to steal not just his keys but his future and his very freedom.

Chapter 18

Satha made good on her ominous declaration two weeks later when, as described before, the North Castle police officers arrived at the house to execute the eviction order that resulted in the police fruitlessly searching for guns in Tom's house and in Tom being evicted, fingerprinted, and forced to spend the night in a seedy hotel. His daughter and dog had, for all intents and purposes, been run out of the house as well after Satha unexpectedly returned to rant and rave so much that the police recommended that Ashley—who still had a legal right to be there—leave the premises as well. The next day, the guns that hadn't been there during the first police search had miraculously appeared, unsecured, on a low-hanging shelf in plain sight.

And since the Judge—the part-time jurist with little courtroom experience of her own—couldn't be bothered to ask the common sense question of how the guns could have gotten there if they hadn't been there the previous night, Tom had found himself essentially homeless and held hostage by the State of New York for a year. His next opportunity to make his case before Judge Lysander was ten days away. All of this had taken place in less than forty-eight hours!

Tom had continued to ask himself, how could a Judge keep him from his home when he had done nothing wrong? This was not only bad: It was, in Tom's opinion, unconstitutional. Moreover, it defied common sense. Sergeant Huffman had said that guns had been found at Tom's home that morning, and they matched exactly the ones Tom had described to him the night before while Officer Scherf searched the premises. Why would any sane person describe the weapons in such detail if he knew they were in plain sight in the house which he had granted the officers the right to search. Never mind that they weren't there the evening before when Tom and the police officers were there. Never mind that the guns had appeared only after Satha was back on the premises. Lord, don't the officers have any common sense, Tom once again thought?

The Judge, when she had finally arrived at the courthouse, also without inquiring into the facts, decided that Tom had lied when he'd told the officers there were no guns at his house. The guns were presumably his and they were not registered as they should have been while in "her" jurisdiction. Therefore, the Judge had decided that this warranted Tom not being allowed to return to his home for a year! A year!

Tom again remembered that as he walked away from that hearing, he had struggled to make sense of what had just happened. He had not been arraigned. He apparently had not been charged with any particular crime. Yet Judge Lysander had taken it upon herself to forbid him from returning to his home through an ex parte issuance of a protective order. Who did she think needed protection? Satha said that she hadn't been threatened and, in fact, if any guns were to be found at the house, she had no idea where they might be. Clearly, Tom was not a danger to anyone wherever the guns were stored.

Tom wondered how he had found himself in this awful situation. Had he done something wrong or was this just terrible luck? Did he deserve to be kept from his home for a year, or was this just the American justice system run amok? Of course, it was the latter. He thought of all the innocent people who are daily convicted, sometimes even executed, for crimes they didn't commit.

Tom understood perfectly well that in California, because of his permit to carry concealed weapons, those firearms that could be carried concealed needed to be registered: That's why he had been sure to renew the registration on his own guns every two years.

Certainly, had Tom known that if any of his weapons were in New York, he would have checked with New York authorities regarding the laws of that state. And, as he was to find out, the registration laws that were at play here only applied in New York City and Westchester County -- and nowhere else in the state of New York. How strange. In any event, he had not known of any of this. He had believed that his guns were out west in the sealed box he had left them in when he had moved away. They should have been with the other boxes that his friend John had stored for him in his house and garage in Encino.

But they were not as it turned out! The police had told Tom that guns fitting the very descriptions of the ones Tom said he owned had been found at the house in Bedford. So how had they gotten there? He once again tried to piece together the story and, finally, with the help of John, was able to do so.

Approximately nine months before, John had found the son of a New York doctor willing to drive Tom's camper to New York so long as all of his expenses were paid. Tom had agreed, and John packed as many of Tom's boxes as could fit in Tom's large 12½-foot camper. John had wanted to clear the boxes from his garage and get them to Tom for safekeeping.

The guns had obviously been in one of the sealed boxes without John realizing it, or he would have alerted Tom. And Tom, busy with Quintessence of Life and his humanitarian work, had not opened any of the boxes since their arrival several months before. Because the Bedford house had been full of furniture and other belongings of Tom by then, Tom had not missed or needed anything that could have been in the boxes stored in the camper. So he had simply left the boxes, unopened, in the camper.

Having stolen the keys to the camper, Satha had obviously gone through the boxes and, in one of them, discovered the guns. Then she or someone at her behest—probably one of the illegal immigrants she would hire from time to time—had taken them into the house and placed them in plain sight on a low shelf in Tom's closet. It was a clever way to set Tom up. In short, she had simply framed him. Was it possible that she actually had already known of the guns when she threatened to "get him"?

Tom realized now his foolishness in not having kept better track of his guns as well as in putting off going through the numerous boxes that had been packed, floor to ceiling, in the camper. But given his clean civic record and high standing in the national community, he had hoped – indeed expected -- that the Judge would have given him a chance to correct the mistake, if a mistake had even been made. After all, he had admitted to Sgt. Huffman that the guns he owned were somewhere and although he thought they were on the west coast, he had also told him that they could conceivably be in the camper and that either officer present had permission to also search there as well as in the house. Nevertheless, Judge Lysander had mandated that he could not return to his home and confined him to the state of New York, thus essentially dispossessing him not only of his guns, but basically of all of his worldly possessions.

Tom did not need to find a copy of the Constitution or google the Bill of Rights to know that he had not been given due process and that several of his constitutional rights had been violated. He already knew that the Fourth Amendment, as amplified by the Fourteenth Amendment, said that no person "shall . . . be deprived of life, liberty, or property, without due process of law" and that Judge Lysander had done just that—deprived him of access to his own home and to essentially all of his property—without even a trial. Tom had not needed to consult a lawyer to know that every level of American government—federal, state, and local—was bound by constitutional law. Yet the Judge had violated Tom's constitutional rights and, in the process, rendered him, his daughter, and his dog homeless. Tom was reminded all too personally of why the Founding Fathers had placed such safeguards in the Constitution: to avoid government overreach and to protect the rights of citizens against an all-too-powerful government.

As Tom tried to determine why the Judge had dealt with him so harshly, he sorted through a number of possibilities. First, there was the matter of how she had come into office. Judge Lysander appeared to have little courtroom experience, and she only presided for approximately one hour at night every other Tuesday. Apparently, she had a small law practice the rest of the time. Perhaps her stern approach was her way of compensating for her limited qualifications for even a low level—the lowest level—judicial position as a part-time Judge of an "inferior court." Tom would never forget the look of exaggerated sternness on her face as she had briefly looked up at him with her glasses shoved down on the bridge of her nose each time he had appeared before her in the courtroom. She had looked up rather than down because the courtroom in Armonk was nothing other than that long table behind which sat the Judge, her clerk, and a bailiff. In front of the table were people appearing before her, largely because of traffic offenses.

When Tom asked his attorney for thoughts on why the Judge was treating him so harshly, Dan suggested that it was possible that because Judge Lysander knew that Tom, before retirement, was an attorney with the highest ratings attainable for both legal competence and for faithful adherence to the highest of ethical standards, as well as being a citizen of substantial standing in the country, she wanted to make an example of him. That's not unusual for small-town elected Judges who want to be in a good position when running for re-election to show how tough they are.

He also remembered learning from Dan that the North Castle Justice Court is, on paper, so insignificant that it is only one of approximately forty village or town courts in Westchester County alone, and Westchester County is but one of sixty-two counties in the state of New York. In all, he had learned that there are close to 1,300 town or village courts in the state, with more than 2,200 Judges of the same rank as Judge Lysander. Their jurisdiction is the lowest of all courts in the state and is primarily concerned with traffic matters, small claims, evictions, local zoning matters, and minor civil matters of less than $3,000. So Tom couldn't understand how Judge Lysander, this part-time Judge of a two-bit court, could dispossess someone of his property. If she could, he was worried about the welfare of the Country because that would effectively mean that the 2nd, 4th, and 5th Amendments and other provisions of the Bill of Rights were no longer worth the paper they were written on. No wonder people are increasingly worried about the direction in which our country has been moving. No wonder stands taken by the NRA, as once explained to him by Charlton Heston, which Tom had historically thought to be far too extreme, were beginning to make more sense.

Whatever the reason for the harsh penalty of removing Tom from his home, Judge Lysander certainly had no sympathy for the former attorney turned humanitarian. She had not stopped to consider the human implications of what she was doing or the way she was upending a man's life as well as that of his daughter. How was Tom or Ashley to go on without access to their computers, files, records, or even their clothes, toiletries, or other possessions? The fact that the "protective order" did not apply to Ashley, in reality it did since she couldn't possibly live safely alone in a house with a crazy person. Tom remembered again thinking about whether he would have enough money to replace the lost effects? Where would he, his daughter, or their family dog even live? Could he sustain the cost of motel bills or a new residence while maintaining financial obligations to the current home he owned and maintained? Tom was thankful that he had the funds to cover many of these costs, but plenty of citizens who might be dropped into his same situation would simply have been unable to manage it.

"What has happened to this country?" he thought. This can't be an isolated incident. Maybe people he had thought to be extremists were actually right. Maybe the government was simply trashing the rights of individuals. Clearly, this was a judicial system run amok!

And it wasn't finished with him yet.

Before he'd left the courthouse that night, Tom had been approached by a seemingly very professional senior officer, Lieutenant Paul Fishman. The Lieutenant said, "You don't have to do this, but would you allow us to take more of your fingerprints? We simply couldn't get a match of the prints on the guns from the prints we took the last time and that makes me, if no one else, very curious."

Lieutenant Fishman continued, "In White Plains, New York, they've got a sophisticated new digital system and it's really state of the art." In fact, according to the Lieutenant, instead of using ink, it used a sort of digital scan of the fingers in order to more accurately capture the image.

"You know, we have no right to request this," Lieutenant Fishman said. "You can say no and we have no real authority to force you to do it, but would you consent to a third set of fingerprints by traveling to White Plains and going through this new process?"

Finally, Tom found his voice. "Yes! Jesus! Of course I will!" he said. "Anything to get it through their heads that my prints are not on the guns," he thought.

The Lieutenant gave Tom the date when he could be fingerprinted for yet a third time. On that day, Tom drove to White Plains. There, Tom met an officer who took the third set of his prints, this time using the new technology, but the result was the same: No match! Once again, the North Castle police were back to square one with regard to their attempts to find Tom's prints on the guns. Although gratified that he was proven right yet again, Tom was unable to take much satisfaction in that fact since they still felt it "unnecessary" to do the obvious: To take the prints of Naar.

The stress of the whole insane situation had begun to get to him. Yes, he had the money to cushion the shock of being turned out of his home and dispossessed—for the moment—of all of his belongings. Unfortunately, money could not cushion Tom's body.

The stress of this ordeal had given him heart palpitations. The shock of having found out that Satha was not a doctor or a professor of anything as she had convincingly claimed had already given Tom one kick in the gut. Now, with the arrest and the eviction, he felt as though he was being pummeled throughout his body each and every day as he struggled to go forward. When the heart palpitations kicked in one night at bedtime while at the motel at which he and his dog were staying, Tom took a trip to a nearby urgent-care physician to make sure that everything was okay. A heart attack was ruled out, but the doctor strongly encouraged Tom to find a way to lessen the stress in his life, as he indeed had an irregular heartbeat and his blood pressure was extremely elevated.

Tom decided that the only thing to do next was to try to get permission to return to his home so he could at least collect some of his possessions.

Chapter 19

Two weeks later, when he returned to Judge Lysander's courtroom at seven o'clock in the evening, Tom was not overly optimistic. Given his previous experiences, he was sure the Judge would deny his request that he have the right to return to his home to retrieve some of his things.

Nonetheless, Judge Lysander surprised Tom and granted him permission. Her lenience came with a caveat, however. Tom would have to have to hire an off-duty police officer to accompany him—completely at his expense—and Tom could only take those things that Satha did not dispute. It was a compromise laden with minefields, as Tom could just imagine the way that Satha would abuse this privilege by disputing every little thing. Tom might leave the home with nothing retrieved at all. Nevertheless, at least he could give it a chance.

On the drive back to Smith Farm Road, Tom felt his shoulders tensing as he imagined the state in which he might find his possessions. All he knew was that, according to his fitness trainer, he had shown up at the house a few days before for his regularly scheduled appointment with Tom, only to find Satha at the door looking guilty and suspicious. Satha had refused to let the trainer in as her eyes kept darting to the left in the direction of Tom's office. Perhaps the trainer was only imagining the guilty look on Satha's face or the way she appeared to be anxious to get him to leave the house. Nonetheless, given the depth of Satha's pathology, Tom worried about the state in which he'd find his affairs.

Upon being let into his house by Satha with the police officer leading the way, Tom learned quickly that he was right to have been worried. He found his office in a frightening state of disarray, with file folders emptied all over the floor, papers in disheveled piles, books knocked off of the shelves, and mail of his which she'd opened splayed out on his desk and on the floor. Tom scooped up all the paperwork he could fit in the box he had brought with him and carried the computer from his desk to the car.

Next, Tom made his way through the remainder of his house beyond the office. As he walked through his bedroom assessing what he hoped to retrieve, Satha followed him around like a yappy puppy who had escaped its leash. The officer at all times walked beside Tom, reminding him that this was a limited visit for a restricted amount of time. This visit was only for the purpose of allowing Tom to take a few items he could carry and primarily those he needed to conduct his business affairs from his motel room. Moreover, he could not take anything with him if Satha uttered the word *disputed*.

Knowing that, Satha repeatedly yelled "Disputed!" to the officer as Tom tried to gather what he could of his possessions. Each time she did so, the officer instructed Tom that he had to leave the item behind, leaving the court to decide later what could and could not be taken.

Next, Tom opened the drawer to his nightstand where he had left the wrapped gift for his daughter the night he had been evicted—a sapphire and diamond ring that had belonged to and been worn by his deceased mother. As Tom removed the small package from the drawer, Satha yelled, "Disputed! That gift was for me!"

"Bullshit," Tom said, unable to keep his calm. "My God, Satha, this was my mother's ring and you know that I planned to give it to Ashley for her birthday."

So the officer said to Tom that he had to move along and have the matter sorted out in some other way. In the meantime, Tom would have to leave without it.

All in all, Tom left the home with very little other than his computer, a small pile of his clothes, and a few critical files that he was able to partially reassemble in a short period of time. Everything else of his that he had expected to take was disputed by Satha, which required Tom to leave it behind.

The visit had been helpful to Tom, but it had certainly been no vindication. He had gotten one of his computers and some of his important office papers. However, his papers were in total disarray, and he'd had to leave all of his cherished personal belongings at the house within Satha's reach. The visit had also left Tom once again feeling violated and hurt as he drove away and contemplated the way in which his life and that of his daughter and assistant seemed to be wrecked further and further with each passing day by the wrongdoing of Satha, by the nonchalance of the North Castle Police Department and, most disturbingly, by the extraordinary overreach by a power hungry small time and small minded Judge who seemingly had no interest in learning the facts of a case before she made life-alternating and transparently wrong decisions.

Of course, he felt yet another wave of anger at Satha. Where had she gotten her sense of entitlement, this belief that she was owed anything she could get her hands on? Wasn't it enough that she had framed him in the first place? As Tom drove the remainder of the way back to his motel room in Mount Kisco, his anger toward Satha was again replaced by even greater wave of anger at Judge Lysander. It was she who had taken Tom's property away from him without due process of law. If she had given him any kind of equitable hearing or instructed the police to do even an elementary follow-up investigation before entering the protective order, he wouldn't be in this situation. What messed up judicial system would allow a part-time small-town Judge to deprive a citizen of such basic constitutional rights?

Had America become a banana republic or, worse yet, a totalitarian state? Tom had begun to wonder if that might actually be the case. Tom felt the hairs on the back of his neck prickle until they spread into a full wave of chills that ran over his shoulders and down his spine. More than any discomfort or loss he felt at the way his own life seemed to be breaking into hardly manageable pieces, Tom was bothered by what this whole circumstance seemed to represent. He thought he could look at this situation one of two ways. He could see it as a one-time incident that had just happened to unluckily befall him. Alternatively, he could see what it really pointed to: the number of Americans whose lives were wrecked each year by Judges like Lysander. The American judicial system, at least in New York, was in the hands of Judges who had been elected or appointed on the basis not of their qualifications or professional competence but their name recognition, their ability to raise money or, depending on the state, their political connections. These folks had no business being in office or sitting in judgment over others who came before them.

Tom was proud to live in a nation where its people had the right to elect most public officials. However, the whole electoral process—not just for the legislative and executive branches but the for judicial branch as well—had become so skewed by campaign financing (and gerrymandering of legislative districts) that it seemed that America's citizens now lived in a plutocracy rather than a democracy. He knew firsthand how individuals without any real knowledge of the Constitution, but just driven by their personal philosophies, were often put into posts because of their connections rather than for their qualifications. Tom was disturbed as he watched his own life and those of others he loved and cared about fall into ruin because a vindictive, greedy, and mentally disturbed person like Satha had not only framed them but had also manipulated and abused the system. However, he was even more disturbed that Judge Lysander, in her inexperience, incompetence, or bias had fallen for Satha's manipulations and issued orders that evidenced that the country he so greatly loved had become one of extreme government overreach and abuse, even at the lowest level.

Chapter 20

When Tom returned to his motel room with the meager belongings he had been allowed to remove from his home, he opened the door to yet another problem. Hercules was no longer in the room! He panicked for a moment, knowing that the motel was not far from a main road and that Hercules might have run loose into traffic. Tom threw his satchel onto the bed and quickly exited the room. He paused a moment to take a calming breath and to remind himself just how smart Hercules was. "Everything is going to be okay," he told himself. Tom walked quickly toward the front desk and breathed a sigh of relief as, even before he got there, he saw Hercules lounging comfortably near the maid in the laundry room.

"Aw, Hercules, bad dog, you come here," Tom said with a joyful smile. He kneeled down and Hercules came over and gave Tom's face a big lick. "You scared me!" Tom said.

As he spoke, the gentleman at the front desk came back to where Tom had found Hercules and said, "He scared us too! He's been running loose all morning and the cleaning ladies are not happy. Neither are our guests. He's a big dog and they are worried he might bite them. Although he's as gentle as can be, our staff doesn't know that and neither do our customers."

"Hercules wouldn't hurt a flea," said Tom.

"Either way, sir," the front deskman continued, "you can't have your dog running loose around the property. You're going to have to control him or move from the premises."

"I will do my best," Tom replied. "He's just so darn smart . . . he knows how to get the door open!"

The deskman wasn't mollified. "Just get it taken care of," he said. "You have one day to solve the problem, or you will have to leave and find other quarters."

Once again, Tom was being threatened with the loss of shelter for himself and his dog. Gritting his teeth, he set about fixing the problem as best he could. At first, he tried to rig up additional ways to keep the door locked, but that only worked while Tom was in the room. As soon as Tom left, Hercules could nudge open the latch of the door bolt with his nose and away he went, wandering through the halls and into the laundry room, making his way to the front desk and scaring the maids and a few timid motel guests in the process. Clearly, the problem wasn't improving. So, although it was a sting to his pride, Tom set about the uncomfortable job of talking to friends to see if they could help him.

Finally, he found what appeared to be a good solution. Some friends of his had a guest house on their property that they were willing to let Tom and Hercules occupy for a few months until their family members arrived to move in. There was just one problem. The house was in Brookfield, Connecticut, and Judge Lysander had forbidden Tom from leaving the state of New York. If he moved in without getting the Judge's permission, Judge Lysander could once again hold him in contempt of court. Who knows what penalty he could face then? He might even get jail time! Tom had no choice but to go back to the Judge and request a hearing for permission to temporarily reside on the property of his truly fine Connecticut friends.

So, on one of the two Tuesdays a month that Judge Lysander held court sessions, Tom was given another hearing. Tom sat in the courtroom and waited his turn to speak, mentally weighing what words he could use to convince the Judge to let him cross the state line to move into his friends' guest house. Hercules would finally have some land on which to roam and Tom would have some space to set up his things, at least for a few months. Together, Tom and Hercules could try to attain some sense of normalcy again. Frankly, they did not have much choice, as the motel had made it clear that Tom and Hercules could not stay any longer.

As for Ashley, she was now in New York City, moving almost night to night from one friend's apartment to another, all the while trying to become gainfully employed. Although she had originally stayed in New Rochelle with Tom's assistant, Natalie, that situation had deteriorated. The stress created by Satha's shenanigans had left Natalie overstressed. Sober and for many years a committed member of Alcoholics Anonymous before the eviction, Natalie had started to drink again as Satha's unlawful action had also made a mess of her life. As a result, Ashley had relocated to New York City, begging couch space from various friends. Just like Tom, she had to rely on the kindness of friends, at least until Tom had stabilized his own situation and could then focus on further helping her.

So on this occasion, when his case was called, Tom stood up in front of Judge Lysander and spoke on his own behalf, with his attorney, Dan, by his side if needed.

"Judge Lysander," Tom began, "I am here to request permission to be allowed to temporarily occupy a residence just across the New York border in Brookfield, Connecticut, where I have some friends who have been kind enough to offer me a place to stay for the next few months. Currently my dog, Hercules, and I are staying in motels in either Armonk or Mount Kisco, and Hercules, who is quite an old dog and weighs over one hundred pounds, continues to get out of the motel rooms and walk into the reception areas, the laundry areas, and throughout the motel premises to such an extent that we have been told that we can no longer stay in the local motels. And I can't just put him in a kennel."

As was her custom, Judge Lysander allowed her glasses to slide down on the bridge of her nose a bit and looked sternly over them to Tom. "Well, surely you can find an alternate place to stay that is within New York," she stated.

Tom explained that this was a unique opportunity for him and Hercules, as the property had several acres where the dog would be free to roam and a separate guest house that would allow both Tom and Hercules to avoid bothering their hosts for the period of time they would be allowed to stay there.

"Well, surely you can find a property with large acreage here on this side of the border," Judge Lysander repeated at least three times.

Before Tom responded, he could not help but think of what he had learned about the Judge before coming to the hearing: that she was not only a part-time Judge but a part-time attorney with very limited trial experience, and perhaps a limited amount of street smarts. Even worse, she reputedly had her own minor criminal record, which had not been brought up when she ran for office. Tom had been told that once she became a Judge she had managed to expunge the incident from the records.

Tom mentally added to the list that, living in Westchester County, she probably came from a privileged background. Perhaps, that was the reason that she was so lacking in empathy or human compassion, not to mention common sense.

Tom, in response to Lysander's question of why not find a place to stay in New York, spoke again. "Well, actually, I don't know anyone around here with that kind of acreage who would also allow me to stay with them. But these friends in Connecticut are both willing and close by. It's not as though I'm going very far away and I will faithfully appear in court anytime you want me to."

Judge Lysander looked down at the table at her stack of folders as she weighed Tom's request. When she looked up, her expression remained stern, but she granted Tom permission to move his residence to Brookfield. "This permission is limited, however," Judge Lysander added. "You may go to and from Brookfield to enter back into New York, but you may not go elsewhere in Connecticut, Vermont, New Hampshire or any other state—none of the surrounding states—without my specific permission."

Tom did not know how to feel, but he was glad to be given authorization to move to a location that was better not only for him but for his dog. At the same time, however, he was appalled that he was still being subjected to something akin to house arrest by this clearly unqualified Judge. It wasn't as though Tom was a criminal. He was an upstanding U.S. citizen who had not committed a crime but who had been framed by a mentally unstable woman for unknowingly allowing his guns to be sent to New York. Even that wasn't a crime. The whole thing was crazy. Fucking crazy!

Yes, he would be able to move into roomier surroundings, but it was still temporary, and it was not his own home, the one he had lived in for the past four years and lovingly taken care of. He was still devoid of most of his belongings too, except for the small number of things he had been able to take away on his last visit, when Satha had disputed almost everything.

Tom thought too of his poor daughter, Ashley, still living with various friends in New York City in a vagabond state. Now that his own residence was taken care of, at least for a few months, Tom was determined to help Ashley find a permanent place to stay.

Chapter 21

The guest home in Brookfield was a welcome change from the motel in Mount Kisco. The friends of his who owned the property knew of many of Satha's failings, and they could not possibly have been more wonderful. That was true of the entire extended family. Although the guest home itself was small, there were several acres on which Hercules could roam, and when he was inside the home with Tom there was room for them both to spread out. Hercules could pick a spot of his choosing to nap, while Tom thought that perhaps he could begin to work on his computer to get his life and affairs back in order as best as he could.

To Tom's dismay, however, he quickly discovered that Satha had ransacked and compromised his computer just as badly as she had ransacked his office and his other belongings. Tom tried to get into each of his accounts, one by one—his bank accounts, his e-mail accounts, his photos, his browser, his music, and his addresses—only to discover that neither his passwords nor answers to security questions worked any longer. Tom finally got back into his accounts at great expense and after three days of work by an IT professional. During that process, the professional had discovered that passwords had been changed to things like Hahaha123 and Stupidfool1000: just more examples of Satha's meanness and madness! The negative consequences of having met Satha seemingly had no end.

The consequences certainly did not end with the changed passwords and hacked computer, although Tom continually tried to stay optimistic and act positively because that was how he had always lived. Tom could no longer travel to do his humanitarian work, but he re-engaged with his nonprofit first via phone and, when finally again working, via his computer. He helped Ashley get set up in an apartment in New York City where she could live on her own until she was able to complete some needed studies and then find new employment. Again, Tom could not himself travel into Manhattan due to Judge Lysander's bizarre protective order, but he could cosign on Ashley's apartment and again help her financially.

There were other things he was able to do, too. Tom resumed a regular exercise regimen at his new residence. This was important to his health, not only because he was getting older but also because he would always be, to some degree, in recovery from the car accident that had previously paralyzed him. The doctors had told him that if his exercise regimen lapsed, some of his former deficiencies were likely to return.

As he returned to a somewhat regular daily routine, Tom also resumed going to medical and dental appointments. To that end, Tom loaded Hercules into the car one afternoon with plans to drop him off at a friend's house for some playtime with the friend's dog while Tom headed into Armonk for a doctor's appointment. After dropping Hercules off, Tom continued on his route to the doctor's office that, of necessity, took Tom down Bedford-Banksville Road, the major arterial in that part of Westchester County. It was a road he needed to travel often, as it was the one that led to town as well as to his doctor's office, to his bank, to his pharmacy, to Hercules's vet, and to most other places he needed to visit from time to time, including the North Castle police station and courthouse located in Armonk.

The thing about Bedford-Banksville Road was that, while it took Tom to the doctor's office he needed to go to that day, it also went relatively close to Tom's own home, the place to which the protective order had forbidden him to go. However, Tom was not worried or even thinking about the proximity of the house to Bedford-Banksville Road on that particular day, as the house itself was set at least two acres back from Bedford-Banksville Road, could not be seen from the road, and in fact could not even be accessed by car from Bedford-Banksville Road. In fact, to even get near to the home's long driveway, much less the house itself, one would first have to turn onto Smith Farm Road and once in front of the house take the long driveway toward the front of the house. Tom understood the protective order to mean that he could not set foot on his property nor could he drive his car onto it. The thought that he should not drive on the main road that led to the side road that led to the driveway that led to the house where Tom was forbidden to go never occurred to him. This was not the first time Tom had driven down this road since the protective order had been issued and he did not think anything of it.

As Tom made his way down Bedford-Banksville Road on this occasion, he wound his way past a particularly dense thicket, a portion of the road that

177

was unpopulated and started humming his favorite tune. It made his heart light to imagine Hercules visiting with his friend Sharon and her dog, also a Weimaraner. With all of Tom's children grown and Ashley only partially needing him now, Tom received much needed joy from his relationship with Hercules. If dog was man's best friend, Hercules was certainly Tom's. No matter what Tom went through, he could always rely on Hercules to be there for him, and Hercules knew he could always rely on Tom, who took him out to walk three times a day, played with him, and let Hercules sleep at the foot of his bed.

Tom rounded another bend that brought him over a hill and sent him gliding down the next stretch of road when he saw something or someone strange standing on the side of the road in the distance. What was that, exactly? Tom's mind told him he was seeing a person, yet the figure was dressed so strangely, in puffy winter outer gear on a fine day and on a busy road without sidewalks where one never saw pedestrians. He slowed his vehicle as he approached the character, who was waving its hands wildly and seemed to be yelling "Stop!" As he got closer, he could see that the figure was Satha, clad from head to toe in Tom's clothing: a winter hat, winter coat, ski pants, and winter moonboots that Tom only wore after a day of skiing.

No other cars were on the road. As Tom approached Satha, he could see that she moved out into his lane, waving her arms feverishly and yelling at him and pointing to his clothing in which she was adorned. God, was she ever sick! For an instant, Tom felt real concern for her. Did she need help? Tom's instinct was to pull the car over and make sure that Satha was okay.

But, instead of stopping, Tom simply slowed down. Satha did not budge from her spot on the road, so Tom slowly moved into the oncoming traffic lane as carefully as he could to avoid hitting her. As Tom passed Satha and looked for her in the rearview mirror, he could see that she was jumping up and down in an agitated way, still trying to get his attention. The caring part of Tom wanted to stop the car to make sure Satha was not in danger, but his logic told him that he must keep going given the protective order that forbade him from going to see Satha or the house. So Tom continued on at a slow pace until Satha had disappeared from view and then he pulled to the side of the road and called his attorney.

He turned off the engine, unclicked his seatbelt, and laid his head back on the headrest while exhaling. My God, that was strange! What on earth was Satha doing in the middle of the road? And why was she there at the exact moment that Tom was driving through there? All Tom could think of was that the doctor's office had called the house to confirm the date and time of Tom's appointment so Satha knew when he would be coming down Bedford-Banksville Road.

It seemed to be one more example of Satha's "good luck": her ability to be in the right place at the right time when it came to causing Tom grief, in the same way that she no doubt had come upon Tom's guns in the camper and been able to use them to frame him in the first place. In any event, Tom's heartbeat slowed back to almost normal as he dialed his attorney to tell him what had just happened. "She was there, waving her arms in the road, trying to get me to stop," Tom explained, "but I just kept on driving."

"Thank God," his attorney replied. "If you had stopped, you would have been in violation of the protective order. No doubt that's what she wanted."

"I feared as much," Tom sighed, "so I just kept driving."

Nevertheless, Tom felt rattled by the whole event and was glad it was behind him—or so he thought.

Chapter 22

The following morning, Tom was sitting at the breakfast table with his newspaper and a cup of hot coffee. He closed his eyes for a moment to enjoy the feeling of the sun streaming through a nearby bay window and warming his face, when his phone rang. It was Sergeant Huffman. "Mr. Strahan," he began, "were you driving down Bedford-Banksville Road yesterday?"

"Yes," Tom replied slowly.

"Well, then, Mr. Strahan, you violated the protective order against you. You'll have to come back in to the police station."

Tom let his head fall back and his eyes gaze up to the ceiling. Dear God, was this really happening?

"But I didn't go to the house," Tom clarified. "I was just driving down Bedford-Banksville Road to get to my doctor's appointment."

"Mr. Strahan," Sergeant Huffman replied, "the house is on the corner of Smith Farm Road and Bedford-Banksville Road, and Dr. Naar has informed us that you drove past it yesterday afternoon. That is right, isn't it?"

"Well, yes," Tom said, feeling suddenly agitated, "but I was on Bedford-Banksville Road, not Smith Farm Road, heading to my doctor's appointment and not going to the house. I *have* to go down that road to get to my physician's office. In fact, I have to go down that road to go to all manner of places that I must visit from time to time: my doctor, the vet, my bank, the market when I shop, my barbershop, and so on."

"Well, Dr. Naar informed us that you drove close to the house yesterday."

"My God," Tom said, losing the usual tone of steadiness that characterized his voice. "I did everything I could possibly do to avoid her! She was standing in the right lane of the road where I happened to be driving and was clearly trying to get me to stop. She had on my jacket and my moonboots that I put on after skiing, something she has never done in her life. I wasn't about to stop so I slowed way down and moved into the oncoming car lane just to avoid her! God only knows how she knew I'd be passing by. A block beyond, I pulled over and called one of my attorneys and told her what the crazy lady had just done."

Tom continued, now trying to gather more information himself. "Did she tell you what on earth she was doing standing in the road? My goodness, as I said, in nice weather she was dressed in a winter hat and coat, waving her arms frantically, obviously trying to get me to stop. Did she tell you any of that? "

"All I know, Mr. Strahan, is that you have violated the protective order by passing the house, and you will have to come into the police station and appear again before Judge Lysander."

"If I have to come in, then I'll come in," Tom said with resignation. "But this seems preposterous to me. I don't understand how driving on a public road, a major one at that, is violating a protective order that states I can't go to a home on Smith Farm Road. What's more, I'd gladly avoid Bedford-Banksville Road if I could, but this is a semi-rural area and it's the only road that leads to most of the places to which I need to go. In fact, I will need to take it to come see you at the police station."

"Oh, don't do that," Sgt. Huffman stated, "or you'll be in violation of the order again."

"This is unbelievable," Tom said. "I'll be in as soon as I can. Just know that it might be a while until you see me, as I have to look at a map to figure out how to get to you without driving down Bedford-Banksville Road."

"Map or no map, Mr. Strahan, please do get here as soon as you can," replied Sergeant Huffman.

The skies had turned gray as morning went on, and a heavy rain started to fall soon after Tom hung up the phone. By the time Tom had consulted a map, packed his briefcase, fed Hercules, and gotten into his car, the rain had worsened. The downpour was so heavy that Tom was unable to make it from the house to his car in the driveway without the bottom third of his pants legs getting wet. He took one last look at the map before starting the car, as he expected he would not be able to consult it while driving, given the sheets of rain that were running down his window.

As Tom slowly made his way down one winding country road after another, he held the steering wheel tightly and strained to see through the windshield, whose wipers could hardly keep up with the rain. Even in good weather, he would have had to drive thirty miles out of his way—almost an hour on these slow-going country roads—to ensure that he could get to the police station without driving on Bedford-Banksville Road. And this was a terrible day to be trying a new route, as visibility was limited and the rain was coming down so hard that it started to flood the roads.

Twenty miles into the trip, the road took Tom to a small wooden bridge that crossed a stream. Tom slowed as he approached, as he could see through a foggy spot on the windshield that he had wiped clean that water was flooding across the bridge and the stream had risen to nearly meet it. Tom stopped the car completely, rolled down his window, and leaned his head out to assess things further. As Tom watched the muddy brown water coursed over the bridge and he could see that the water level was rapidly rising. He thought about whether he should try to cross the bridge anyway. If he had to back up, it would add an unknowable amount of time to this already long trip. But as Tom sat there in his car, the base of the bridge disappeared before his very eyes. The bridge had completely washed out! He had no choice but to turn around and find yet another way.

By the time Tom arrived at the police station, his nerves were in a jangle. It had taken him almost two hours to drive what should have been a thirty-minute trip, his car was splattered with mud, and though he was wearing a raincoat his pants were soaked from the walk into the station. He could hardly stand to learn what was going to happen next now that he had been told he had violated the protective order.

Sergeant Huffman explained that Judge Lysander had been called to come in for another special hearing to handle Tom's case. The police were not going to rearrest Tom, thank God. However, Judge Lysander decided to extend the protective order further, from one year to a year and a half! According to her, Tom had indeed violated the order by driving on the Bedford-Banksville Road which went close to the Smith Farm Road property, even though the house itself was set back very far from the road, could not be seen from the road, and the only entry to the property was from another road entirely.

Upon hearing the news that he was now forbidden to return to his home for a year and a half, Tom found himself wanting to yell fiercely into the space of the small gray courtroom so that his voice reverberated off of the cinder block walls and pierced Judge Lysander's ear drums. Tom was not a violent or impatient man, so to have the urge to yell said something. Tom was as close to his limit as he had been since this whole judicial ordeal had begun. "Just how fucked up can a system be?" he thought. "Things can't possibly get any worse."

And then they did. Later that same day, Tom received a phone call from his lawyer informing him that the Westchester County district attorney had been alerted by Satha of Tom's alleged violation of the protective order and they now had serious concerns over the situation. The DA's office was considering pressing charges against Tom for having unregistered guns in Westchester County. Having unregistered guns could technically be considered a felony although, according to Tom's lawyer, this was true only in New York City and, conveniently enough, Westchester County, and not elsewhere in the state of New York. If found guilty, Tom could theoretically be sentenced to prison.

Tom hung up the phone in a sort of daze. He walked robotically into the front room of his small temporary home and fell onto the couch so that his eyes looked up toward the ceiling. And, as he now had so many times before, he went through the same mental process that just played over and over and over in his mind: What kind of woo-woo world had he become ensnared in? Was he even living in the United States of America anymore, the country where every defendant was guaranteed a fair trial by the Constitution? How could a part-time village Judge continue to unilaterally take away Tom's property without the benefit of a trial, whatever the charge? This tyrannical approach to administering "justice" was incomprehensible to Tom who, before retirement, had been admitted to practice law in over ten states.

Such thoughts had now played so many times in his mind that Tom was beginning to question the well-being of the citizenry of his very own country in light of extreme overreach and intrusions by the government into the daily lives of all Americans. Seemingly, it was no longer the United States in which he had grown up and, for the first time in his life, he began to understand the feelings of some Americans with whom he had never before agreed. Is it people like Lysander that are driving people to take what, to him, had always before been considered extreme positions?

He wondered long and hard about that, and about a conversation he had long, long ago with Charlton Heston. People are generally more complex and multi-faceted than most people give them credit for and that was certainly true of Heston. In all likelihood, the majority of people who remember Heston think of him solely as some sort of right-wing kook, all based on the iconic photograph of him holding a rifle in his hand saying that it would have to be pried from his cold, dead hand. However, although Tom did not agree with what he thought to be Heston's extreme views on the 2nd Amendment, he knew Heston to be a very deep thinker and quite progressive on most issues of our time. After all, he

186

was committed to civil and human rights, had marched with Martin Luther King, Jr., and had a heightened sense of environmental awareness. His view was that, although our country could certainly be harmed by terrorist attacks of one kind or another, we could never be successfully invaded or occupied. He argued that we had been blessed to be bordered to the east and west by two great oceans, to the north by an advanced but friendly and small (from the standpoint of population) nation, and by a weak nation to the south. No, that was not the cause of his positions on gun control. Rather, they were founded on what he believed to be the real threats to our liberties, and those threats came not from outside but from our own government. He argued that was why the Founding Fathers had established a system of checks and balances that served us well for the better part of 200 years, but given the world in which we now live might no longer be up the task. Thus, to prevent a tyrannical government takeover, it was necessary that we be prepared at all times to protect ourselves from the real danger – our own government that was becoming increasingly oppressive.

Although Tom had not accepted what he thought to be exaggerated views of Heston at the time, he was beginning to rethink his own views in light of what had happened to him over the last several months. If one of the lowest level Judges In the country could take not only his guns, but his home and all of his personal possessions without him even being convicted of a crime, then it would be easy for authorities to disarm and make defenseless every single person in the nation. In this event, however unlikely, the Army, the National Guard and/or local law enforcement agencies, and possibly all of the above working in concert with each other could "take over" the nation without ever firing a shot. Although this thought might seem to be preposterous on its face, the more Tom thought about it, the more he came to the realization that the danger was just that real. This was scary shit and Tom would give much thought to it, probably for the rest of his life. Lysander's actions caused a change of mind when all others had failed.

Chapter 23

On the surface, the problem was not only Lysander, but also obviously Satha who, after framing Tom, kept calling the police and Tom had now learned, the district attorney as well—Satha, who had obviously found Tom's guns as some sort of sick bit of serendipity, taken them into the house, and placed them in plain sight on a low shelf in Tom's closet. As crazy as she was, she clearly had either a sympathetic or biased Judge and a police force willing to listen to her blather over and over again without ever looking into her veracity.

Yet, as much as Satha's behavior enraged Tom, it was the criminal and judicial system that Tom, as a retired attorney – the early years as a prosecutor -- and an acknowledged constitutional scholar, could see was the far greater menace. After all, Naar was just a sick and evil criminal, but the police agency and the court system of North Castle was quite a different matter. The police and the DA were fielding calls and complaints from a woman and responding to them without ever investigating the credibility or mental state of the woman. They weren't even using common sense to evaluate the elements of the case: fingerprints that didn't match those on the guns; the guns appearing in plain sight the morning after the house was searched with negative results; a constitutional scholar giving consent to a search of the house, something no one would have done if he knew that guns were in the house. It shouldn't take police training—just common sense—to conclude that this didn't pass the "smell test." Moreover, just a modest amount of detective work would have revealed that Satha was a mentally unstable woman with a long history of lies, deception, and, indeed, criminal conduct. Even if the police had not done their due diligence, if Judge Lysander had given Tom a hearing, Tom and multiple witnesses familiar with Satha's history of fraud and criminality could have made a compelling case against her, one that would surely have convinced any fair-minded person of his innocence and of her lies and false accusations.

But with the situation having now escalated to the point that the DA could conceivably press felony charges, Tom and his attorney, Dan, once again met at the same Pine Cone Café they had met in many months before to discuss the best way to proceed. They sat at a small table in the back of the wood-paneled coffee shop and were sure to keep their voices low so they would not be heard above the din of customers chatting and the baristas steaming coffee.

Tom didn't say much at first, as he was still reeling from the news, trying to understand how he might—even though unlikely-- end up in prison. His guns had all been acquired lawfully—all as gifts, for goodness' sake!—and were properly registered in the state in which Tom had believed them to be. Tom had not carried or used any firearm in over forty years. The fact that the police had confiscated his gun collection altogether was something he apparently had to accept even though, in his opinion, it was clearly a violation of his Second Amendment rights. But to attain a criminal record and possibly even be sent to prison would obviously be a gross injustice given no wrongdoing on Tom's part, his clean background, and his history of community and humanitarian service. Yet he had become all too familiar with the Westchester County "justice" system. By this time, he knew all too well that anything was possible.

In his years as a trial lawyer, Tom had seen many times that a district attorney who was up for re-election would pick certain cases to "win," usually by way of a plea bargain, so that he or she could have a trophy showpiece to hold up to constituents in the lead-up to an election. It's possible that the Westchester County DA was zeroing in on Tom's case given that Tom was a person of some notability. He was known throughout the country for his representation of high-profile clients, for his reputation as a constitutional scholar, and for his record of successfully trying First Amendment and complex antitrust cases. No DA wanted to be criticized for giving special treatment to a celebrity or to a person whom some might perceive to be newsworthy.

Yet Tom's notability might be used to convince the DA not to charge Tom with a felony, or with any crime for that matter. On the one hand, the DA would look good if he could publicize the conviction of a particularly visible and reputable person like Tom. On the other hand, an acquittal could make the DA look foolish and mean-spirited. Lost votes during an election could follow.

Dan raised this possibility with the DA's office in an effort to convince them to back off. Simultaneously, he hatched an idea that he shared with Tom the next time they spoke on the phone. He wondered if Tom would be willing to enter into a non-criminal disposition of all matters. Tom wanted to know what Dan had in mind.

"We could get all of this behind you and the DA could get out of this sticky situation if you agreed to what we call a 240 disposition," Dan explained. "It's not a plea to either a misdemeanor or a felony. It's a non-criminal violation akin to a traffic citation. Moreover, the files and records are to be sealed.

"Why take a chance on anything?" continued Dan. "You have a Judge with a thorn in her butt, a lazy and indifferent police department, and an unpredictable DA. Let's just put all of this behind you."

Tom found the suggestion distasteful. Dan knew that Tom would never, never enter a plea to any kind of crime, no matter how minor. Tom carefully read the statutory provision to which Dan referred. Dan's explanation seemed to be correct and his reasoning sound. Tom would have much preferred to have a fair trial that allowed him to establish that he had not violated the protective order by driving down Bedford-Banksville Road and that he had not even been aware that the guns had been brought into New York state which, by itself, was not even a crime. After all, this is the United States of America isn't it? And the Interstate Commerce Clause and other provisions found in the Constitution provide for free movement between states.

But then, as Tom made another one of his long, circuitous trips from his temporary home in Brookfield back to Westchester County to take care of errands while avoiding Bedford-Banksville Road, a new insight opened up for him. He wanted to go home: not back to the home of which he was a Tenant-in Common owner in Bedford, but back west to a part of the country he had always loved and where he had lived virtually his entire life. In addition, he was sick of Westchester County, with its sorry system of injustice masquerading as justice. He was tired of tripping the wires on Satha's landmines. And he was tired of living in a part of the country that, while beautiful, was owned an enjoyed by just a few—the elite who could afford to buy the land and parcel it off for themselves on multi-acre lots.

Tom had come to New York for an adventure, and he had gotten more than he wanted or deserved. He had thought all along that if things with Quintessence of Life did not work out, he could always move on. That time had clearly come. And yet Tom remained tethered to New York state, tethered to Westchester County, tethered to the North Castle police station and courthouse, and thus tethered to the unstable, duplicitous, and truly devious Satha.

If only for his physical and mental wellbeing, Tom had to get out of this place. He called Dan to tell him that he would be willing to agree to the 240 disposition as long as nothing about the charge would ever be noted or considered criminal in nature, the files would be sealed, and on condition that Tom would be allowed to leave the state and the region so he could move back west—and the sooner, the better!

Chapter 24

The DA's office, apparently not quite sure what to do and being convinced that Tom would never enter a plea to any kind of criminal charge, no matter how minor, ultimately presented Tom with the chance to agree to the 240 non-criminal consent decree that was the equivalent of a traffic violation. After yet further consideration and at the recommendation of his attorney, Tom did finally agree to the consent decree in order to avoid the time, expense, and unpredictability of a trial on any kind of criminal charge. However, before doing so, Tom set forth with Lysander all of the conditions set forth in his prior discussions with his attorney.

As good as it might have looked for the DA to have a win to showcase during the next campaign season, apparently the possibility of an acquittal of a seventy-year-old respected constitutional scholar and international humanitarian was far too worrisome for the D.A.'s office to take the risk. The end result of the negotiation with the D.A.'s office was that the protective order would remain intact for the remainder of its period, but that Tom would now have permission to leave the region and, thus, he would no longer be a detainee of New York State. Instead, he could travel as he pleased and relocate back out west. Tom also demanded as part of the non-criminal consent decree that all files and records in the North Castle court be sealed so that no potential misunderstandings or issues would ever trail Tom as he got on with his life. The court agreed and promised that all court documents would be sealed.

While it was hard to be happy about anything related to Judge Lysander or the judicial ordeal through which he had gone, Tom did feel relieved to finally have permission to leave the area and the freedom to move back west. He would not yet have full closure with the issue of Satha, as he remained the tenant-in-common owner of the home that Judge Lysander had forbidden him to visit. But he could at least disentangle himself from the dysfunctional criminal justice system of Westchester County.

Tom strongly suspected that the personnel at the North Castle police station and courthouse would be equally happy to get rid of him after his case had been resolved. Over the weeks and months that Tom had interacted with them, he had watched their initial cordiality wane. They were tired of dealing with both Tom and Satha and seemed to simply wish that they and their problems would just go away. There was a continual tendency for the police to simply say that matters in dispute were out of their jurisdiction and should be handled by the civil courts. "We'll let the civil court handle that" was a common refrain used as a sort of pass for Judge Lysander and by the North Castle law enforcement officers in order to avoid further responsibility. Tom was well aware of various—although not all—law enforcement officers simply passing the buck to someone else or kicking the proverbial can down the road to get matters off of their desks and out of their purview.

Tom was deeply bothered by the way Judge Lysander and the police at the North Castle station would curtly route issues to the civil court whenever they could find an excuse to do so. It was not as though Tom wanted to be in this mess, and yet the fatigue in the eyes of the police personnel at the station whenever Tom appeared had become pretty much "you again?"

One intake officer at the front desk was particularly out of order one day when Tom and Ashley arrived to file lengthy typed affidavits on the topic of Satha's theft of their property. The affidavits were quite detailed, consuming multiple typewritten pages. However, the young officer wrongfully said that typed affidavits could not be submitted even if signed in his presence under oath, and that, as such, they had to be handwritten in their entirety. That was simple balderdash and was really nothing other than harassment, as a higher ranking officer later confirmed to Tom. In any event, Tom, whose handwriting had never fully recovered after the car accident, sat down in the police station, chastened, and took an hour and a half to rewrite the entire document that he had already painstakingly typed out.

Finally, having agreed to the non-criminal 240 disposition, Tom requested the return of his guns from the North Castle Police Department. The officer with whom he spoke told him that the guns had been "destroyed" many months before. "That is absolute baloney, complete malarkey," said Tom. He knew from years of work with law enforcement agencies that any evidence of possible criminal wrongdoing or that might be needed as evidence in a later trial would always be kept in an evidence locker. Once again he was being taken for a fool. He was as certain as anyone could be that his weapons were now in the

197

"private" collections of various officers, and there wasn't anything he could really do about it.

If the North Castle police thought "good riddance" of Tom, he most certainly thought "good riddance" of them as well. It was sad that their interactions had to be marked by such distaste, given all of the wonderful and close relationships Tom had had with law enforcement personnel and Judges over the course of his life. But this seemed to be the way things had to be, and Tom was more than ready to extricate himself from this toxic environment.

Tom would, however, have to have one more interaction with the North Castle police. It was the day Tom was set to move his truck and his camper back west. He had been granted permission by the court to remove his large cab-over camper from the property on Smith Farm Road. As had been the case the last time Tom had been to the property to remove a few of his things, he had to hire an off-duty police officer to accompany him to his own property to ensure that Tom did not bother Satha or break the law in any way, as the protective order was still in effect.

For several months, Tom had not had a set of keys to the camper, as Satha had taken them the day she had moved out of the house while saying, "I am going to get you, and I know how to do it!" Nevertheless, Tom had finally been able to obtain a duplicate key to the back door of the camper from his friend John, with whom Tom had left a key when he first went east.

Greg, another friend of Tom's, flew east from Los Angeles to New York City to assist Tom in his cross-country relocation. So Greg, Ashley, Tom, and another hired police officer went to the Smith Farm Road property with the Super Duty F-350 one-ton truck to pick up the camper itself.

However, first things first: They had to load the camper onto the truck. There were a number of power sources and cords right inside the nearby garage door. But Satha had changed the locks and the garage door wouldn't open. This was critical, because the four hydraulic legs of the camper wouldn't lift without power. Finally, they were able to manually get the camper onto the truck bed.

The plan was that Tom would take Hercules and head west as soon as possible in order to be at the home Tom had rented in Santa Monica before movers Tom had hired arrived at the home. After loading the camper onto the truck, Greg was going to take Ashley to New York City and then go on to Philadelphia for a short visit with his parents before embarking on his own cross-country journey in the truck and camper. So, unlike Tom, Greg was under no time constraints.

Tom approached the camper to unlock it. As he did so, he thought about all of the things that he loved about this cross-country vehicle, which he hadn't been inside of since it had been driven cross-country by the doctor's son.

The camper was really deluxe. It was nice when he bought it, but thereafter he had added a number of features: refrigeration, an oven, a microwave, a juicer, a TV, and a surround-sound music system. It slept eight and had both a flush toilet and a shower inside and a generator as well. With Tom's lifelong love of exploring, it was perfect. The camper had seen Tom through many miles of travel, allowing him to crisscross the country from Maine to the shores of the Pacific and everyplace in between. He especially loved having the camper because it gave him the ability to go when and where he wanted to go and to stop where and when he chose as long as it was in a public and lawful place.

So Tom took one step up to the back entry of the camper and jiggled the key in the lock as the officer stood a few paces behind him. The key turned after a few tries. Tom turned the handle and pushed the door open. As he did so, even before he could see the mess, a putrid stench of mildew and mold pierced his nose. "My God," Tom gasped.

He took a single step into the camper but no more, as the rank odor kept him at bay. It was starting to get dark, but with a large and powerful flashlight, Tom was able to survey the interior, trying to make sense of what he was seeing. The storage boxes, once packed neatly with some of Tom's financial records, books, photo albums, and computer discs, were all gone. Needless to say, so were the boxes containing the guns that, by this time, were known to have obviously been in the camper, as they had to have been placed there by his friend John before the camper had been driven east.

Everything that remained was waterlogged. Grayish black mildew and mold had sprouted on all of the surfaces as well. Yes, mold and mildew had overtaken the entire camper.

Tom knew instantly that Satha had caused this destruction to happen. Clearly Satha, who had never camped a day in her life, had taken a hose and hosed down everything inside the camper. As she or more likely someone she hired had already removed the boxes and their contents, the rest of the interior she had soaked including the beds, benches, walls, and ceiling. After that, she'd apparently sprayed the kitchen appliances and media center. What a crazy bitch!

After taking a moment to collect himself, Tom called out, "Officer, can you come in here?" As the officer came over Tom said, "It's a disaster in here. The whole inside has been absolutely soaked with water."

With the rancid smell now evident even outside and at ground level, the officer declined to enter. He said he didn't need to as he could not only smell it but could see that the interior was a mess without going inside. The officer rubbed the back of his head, running his hands along his buzzed stubble, as if uncomfortable and not sure what else to say.

Tom already knew that Satha had gotten her hands on his guns, removed them from one of the boxes, and taken them inside before calling the police. Now Tom could see with his very own eyes that Satha had also gotten her hands on his other things that John had placed in the camper months before. Having seen the way she operated, he had no doubt that by now she would have stolen anything of value that she found in the boxes. Whatever was left, she had found a way to ruin. She had saturated the place with water, which was nearly as damaging as setting it on fire.

Disheartened by what he'd seen of the interior, Tom then climbed back down in order to see if he could detect the extent of the camper's damage on the outside. He walked the perimeter of the camper as he thought about exactly how Satha had managed to ruin his things. As he approached the back of the vehicle, his eyes fell upon a green garden hose. Satha had had the bravado—or was it laziness? —to leave the hose just a few paces away from the camper. The image of her standing with hose in hand, spraying down the interior of his $100,000 camper, sickened Tom.

"Did you see the speakers in there?" Tom said to the officer. "Surround sound. I used to listen to Frank Sinatra's 'My Way' and other classics when I'd drive from California to another part of the country. I'm sure they no longer work."

"You think?" the officer said, trying not to be pessimistic.

"You saw it in there," Tom replied. "Everything's been soaked. She"—Tom pointed toward the house, meaning to reference Satha—"ruined everything."

"Do you still want me to drive the truck and camper?" Greg asked. "Is it even worth getting back home so you can try to salvage it?"

"My God, I have over $100,000 invested in the camper," Tom said. "I don't know how much of that can be salvaged, but I certainly want to try. As long as the cab of the truck is suitable for you to sit in while driving and you can safely drive, let's stick with the plan."

"Okay," Greg said, still optimistic. "I'll check it out."

Tom felt grateful to see that even when one human being was punching him in the gut, another was treating him with kindness and consideration. Tom was not ready to give up on human nature, and he resolved never to do so.

Once Tom and Greg sorted through various remaining issues with the camper, Tom wished Greg well and watched Greg and Ashley, whom Greg was taking into New York City before going on to Philadelphia, maneuver the truck and camper out of the driveway. It was a beast of a vehicle, but Greg seemed to have the experience to drive it, at least at five miles an hour.

Earlier that same day, a moving truck that Tom had hired had arrived at a storage unit Tom had rented several months before. As night approached, the movers had put the last piece of Tom's furniture, the items Satha had apparently not wanted, in the moving truck. After having Tom sign some paperwork, the movers had said a quick good-bye and then headed out to start the long drive to the house in Santa Monica, California that Tom had rented.

Tom had every intention of beginning his journey west that evening as well, but forty-five minutes into the ride, he discovered that he was simply too tired to continue driving. Therefore, he checked in to a motel for the night and left a voice mail for Greg telling him where he would be staying. Although Tom had used prudence in getting some sleep, he had foremost in mind that he needed to arrive in Santa Monica before the movers. If he was not there, they would move on to another person's moving job and maybe, for an extra fee, circle back to Tom's at their convenience.

Just as Tom was drifting off to sleep in his motel room, his cell phone rang. He did not recognize the number but, after a moment, he recognized the voice. It was Greg.

"Tom, I just got to Manhattan thirty minutes ago," he said. "It was a nightmare of a drive. I couldn't accelerate past thirty-five miles an hour, and every car on the freeway was passing me by."

"What happened?" Tom asked.

"The camper was so waterlogged that I simply couldn't make it go any faster. Worse yet, I couldn't control it. A police officer stopped me and told me the obvious: that it's not safe to have the vehicle on the road. He demanded that the camper be taken off the road first thing in the morning."

Tom's heart sank. He had already lost so much at the hands of Satha: years of his life; hundreds of thousands of dollars of unpaid business loans; mementos and valued items that she had stolen from him, including his guns; being framed by her; and now this. Tom knew that things were just things, but it still made him sad to imagine letting the camper go as well. He took a deep breath and said, "Okay, if it can't be driven, it simply must be abandoned or demolished." He made plans with Greg to dispose of the camper first thing in the morning, thanked him profusely for his time and help, and slipped back under his bed covers. It took an hour of tossing and turning before he could fall asleep.

Very early the following morning, Tom and Greg met up and located a waste disposal site not far away. Greg drove the truck and camper slowly to the facility, with Tom following closely behind in his SUV. The operators at the site had never seen a large cab-over camper collapsing around and onto a truck due to its waterlogged condition. It took over an hour to have it removed by huge cranes that were necessary to pry it off the truck. Then a crusher was brought in to completely crush the camper. It reminded Tom of the scene in the movie *Goldfinger*. Good-bye, camper—forever.

Chapter 25

By this time, the moving truck had already gotten a significant jump start on Tom, and he now needed to make up the time so he could try to beat the movers to Santa Monica.

It was important to Tom to have the furniture and household goods that he had been allowed to remove from his Bedford home transported in the moving truck on their own without being jumbled together with items from other people's household moves. He knew from past moves and other people's horror stories how botched a moving job could become if the moving company combined the goods from more than one client in the same truck. If boxes were not properly labeled by the company and incredible attention was not paid by the movers at unloading time, household goods from one family could easily get mixed up with those of another and end up being delivered to the wrong place. Once incorrectly delivered, it becomes very difficult to track down lost items, whether because the moving company cannot locate where the boxes had ended up due to poor record keeping or because the family receiving the wrong boxes had not noticed that boxes had been incorrectly delivered if the boxes in question had been left sitting in the garage or the basement gathering dust with other things not yet unpacked.

As a result of his concerns, Tom had gotten the movers to commit to moving his things to his new home without crowding in goods from anyone else's move. But the deal was that Tom would be at his new home to let the movers in. If he was not, they had permission to go on to the next moving job, where they would load additional boxes into the moving truck, where Tom's goods already were. Tom had already lost so much to Satha and the so-called justice system of Westchester County that he felt he just didn't want to endure more of his personal goods getting abused, mixed up, or lost. In striking the atypical arrangement with the movers to move Tom's things on their own, Tom felt that he was finally winning back some control in his life. He comforted himself with the notion that maybe, just maybe, in moving back west and doing it on his own terms, he would be turning a corner on the past year and a half and entering into something better—a lot better!

So very early the following morning, Tom showered and dressed quickly at the hotel at which he had stayed, dropped his key card at the front desk, and went out to the parking lot with Hercules on a lead behind him. The other cars in the lot stood silently, as their owners probably were still asleep inside their respective rooms. Tom, who had grabbed a cup of coffee on his way out of the reception area, was now feeling wide awake. The electricity of knowing that he had to get to his new home before the movers did, as well as the lack of a full night's sleep had him buzzing – with the help of the coffee no doubt.

Tom wound his way through the curving back roads of New York State as he headed west across New Jersey into Pennsylvania and started to feel the stress mount. He'd be damned if he'd let the movers beat him to his house, and yet he could only go so fast without getting the attention of patrolmen. Making matters worse, a local pickup truck full of loose building supplies had pulled out in front of him, and now Tom was stuck tailing him at ten miles an hour slower than the speed limit. Just when Tom felt like he couldn't take the stress of racing against the clock any longer, the road opened up into multiple lanes and the speed limit increased. Hercules gave a low groan as if he understood that something had changed; perhaps it was merely Tom's acceleration that had triggered it, but Tom felt sure that Hercules was rooting for him. As the road opened up, so did the great expanse of Tom's mind. Although he did not let up on the gas pedal, Tom felt himself traveling more fluidly now that he was out from behind the slow pickup and on a major road, which soon gave way to a scenic stretch of the Interstate Highway System.

As the highway entered Ohio, Tom felt a great weight melt off of his shoulders. Freedom! After so many months of being a detainee of New York State, Tom was free to travel the country and the world. No corner of the globe had ever been too remote for Tom to visit and explore, and the idea that he could now return to the way of life that was so much his own was invigorating. That's not to say that world travel was all he had missed. Tom was an American, through and through, and he had longed to again set foot in some of his favorite places in the west: Yosemite, Yellowstone, the Grand Canyon, and others; places that were on a grand scale like no other places in the world; places where he could exercise his legs and lungs, breathe and move, and roam with Hercules. Tom had moved to California from Kentucky by way of Texas with his parents and brother when he was twelve years old, but he had lived in California for most of his adult life, and now he was returning to the area with which he most identified and that he most loved.

The home that he had rented was a modest one, yet it had everything that Tom needed. There was a cathedral ceiling and wall shelves where he could display mementos and awards from various foreign and domestic countries and states. He was absent whatever Satha had kept, and the retrieval of those items if they even still existed, would have to wait until another day. He would simply have to remain positive. Besides, the move back west would give him proximity to the kind of outdoor activities that Tom most loved—biking, tennis, kayaking, hiking, and skiing—and ensured that Tom would be able to get out and stretch his legs again. Many of his old friends would be waiting for him there too, people who had known him for many years and who would never question his integrity in the way that had been done in the past year and a half because, quite simply, they truly knew him.

Tom was grateful to have escaped Westchester County without having had a major health crisis either. All of those months fighting while trying to demonstrate his innocence, to put his life back together, and to handle not being allowed to move beyond the region of Westchester County—not even to Manhattan, just an hour away—had taken their toll on him. Looking in the mirror, Tom was sure he looked older, with certain of his gray hairs having turned white and new wrinkles cropping up around his eyes. Although he had done his best to keep up his exercise regimen, he had found that being displaced from his home, occupied with the legal hassle of being repeatedly detained, and limited in where he could travel had cramped his ability to get outdoors and exercise his body. His blood pressure had gone up, and his doctor had ordered him to watch his salt intake to see if that would make a difference. Tom knew his blood pressure had nothing to do with salt, however, as he didn't over consume in that regard. It had to do with stress brought on by a wily and Machiavellian woman and an addled and power-crazed part-time Judge sitting in a tiny village.

And as the long miles unfolded between Westchester County and St. Louis on the way back to California, Tom could almost feel his blood pressure lowering. He was free, he was alive, and he was ready to start the next phase of his life, with renewed possibilities awaiting him.

* * * * *

Tom drove straight through, clear across the country, with only short naps and one motel night in between. Whether it was due to his focused driving or divine intervention, Tom pulled into the driveway of his rental home before the moving truck arrived. Having spoken to the drivers by phone earlier in the day, Tom knew that they were now approximately one hundred miles behind him. They were required by their company home office to take mandatory sleep breaks of reasonable length, which were certainly longer than those Tom had taken.

Tom clapped his hands together and looked at Hercules in the backseat. "Herc, we're home!" he said with a grin. He swung his legs out of his seat into the open air, where he could breathe in the fresh scent of the Pacific Ocean, which was not far away.

In a matter of hours, his good friend John showed up, as did the moving company, and together they brought in Tom's things. Once the couch was placed in Tom's new living room, Tom and John plopped down on it and had a very long chat.

They spoke of many things: of all that Tom had been through in the past year and a half, of the way that the justice system in America had deteriorated, and of the manner in which the judiciary system had seemed to become an ideological bastion for both Republicans and Democrats rather than a fair and objective system designed to protect the civil rights of American citizens as the Founding Fathers had intended.

"You know, in confidence," Tom shared, "I have a friend who was appointed to the United States Supreme Court after having failed the California bar exam several times. He's a really nice guy, but he was not chosen because he was qualified, God bless him, but simply because he was trusted to represent the ideals of his political party and to protect the interests of the President who had appointed him."

"Shit," John said, "that's outrageous. How can we trust our highest court in the land if we cannot be assured that those appointed to serve are not objective, trustworthy, and qualified?

"That's really worrisome," John continued, "but forgive me for not understanding how your story, at the local level, is not just the case of singular incompetence or bias on the part of one small-town justice and some bad luck on your part."

"My God, John, let me tell you the ways that this is a widespread issue," Tom said. "Judicial qualifications and objectivity are imperative at all levels, from the highest court in the land to the lowest. We learn almost daily of people who have been wrongfully convicted of criminal conduct—some even executed—for crimes they demonstrably didn't commit.

"Injustices on the civil side are just as rampant, though the consequences may not be as severe. This is especially true in states where Judges are simply elected and, as a result, judicial qualifications and temperament hardly come into play. Those seeking Judgeships often do so for purposes of prestige or because they aren't very successful at practicing law. In other words, they are like any other politician out there raising money, generally from special interests, and doing whatever they can to get name recognition. That's a hell of a way to run a railroad, isn't it?

"I love my country, John, you know I do. But I'm scared about its future. If we don't learn from past mistakes, we are bound to see them repeated," Tom finished.

Chapter 26

Having returned to California, Tom began to sort out his life. He went about unpacking his things, including hanging up a weave painting that he had purchased in Vietnam. The artist was a young, deaf, horribly disfigured, and disabled man who could only use one hand and his feet. Tom put the piece of art on the wall near the foot of his bed so that every morning when he awoke, he could be reminded that no matter what kind of hardships came his way, he had all of his faculties to be thankful for. He was still capable of making contributions to his community and of doing great things.

Tom also got whatever papers and documents he had in order and reengaged his nonprofit and humanitarian endeavors with a new vigor and sense of purpose. This included trips abroad to Asia and Latin America, where he commenced again working to help people in rural and often remote parts of the developing world.

The first trip out of the country went fine for Tom, but the moment that Tom set foot back on U.S. soil, he ran into trouble in the airport. After standing in the long immigration line with his travel companions, Tom stepped up to the booth to have his passport checked. Tom smiled at the gentleman running his passport through the computer and waited to be released as he had been on scores of other trips when he returned to the United States.

"Excuse me, sir, but I'm not going to be able to let you through right now. I need you to speak with my supervisor," the officer said. "You'll have to wait here until he arrives."

"What's wrong?" Tom asked, confused. Tom's traveling companions were confused as well, as they had been quickly processed through immigration and were waiting for Tom.

After a wait of close to thirty minutes, another officer came up. "I'm going to need to escort you over to the holding room," the officer said, again without providing additional detail.

"But why?" Tom asked in disbelief. "You know, I have a connecting flight that I'm sure to miss if you keep me here much longer. And my travel companions are right there, waiting for me!"

"Regardless," the officer said, "this is what has to be done. You may tell your companions you have to stay behind and they should go on, but now I need to get you into an office over on the other side of immigration."

Tom had been accompanied on this particular overseas trip by socially responsible colleagues, and he was on especially congenial terms with these individuals. As a result, he found this circumstance to be incredibly embarrassing. "Why don't you all go ahead?" Tom suggested. "It appears there is some kind of a problem in the system. I assume I have been randomly selected for further review. Anyway, I have to stay behind awhile to get it resolved. I'm sure it's just a glitch, but I don't want to hold you up."

Tom's friends expressed their concern and one of them even offered to stay behind, but Tom insisted that they go on lest they too end up missing their connecting flight. Tom waved them off and returned to the immigration officer who was standing just a few yards away from him, at attention, ready to take Tom into his custody and walk him over to the special office he had earlier referenced. That is, indeed, what the gentleman did, and Tom proceeded to sit in the cold waiting room for another forty-five minutes before yet another supervisor finally showed up.

When the supervisor finally did arrive and looked at a computer screen for only a moment or two, he said, "You need to get that matter in New York cleared up or you'll be stopped every time you re-enter the country."

"What matter in New York?" asked Tom. "The only matter pending in New York is a civil case in which I am the plaintiff. Can you tell me what you're seeing on your screen?"

"No, sir, I'm not at liberty to say, although it was posted by a court in the county of Westchester, New York," the man said. "You're free to go, but again, I encourage you to get the matter cleared up with the involved court."

Tom was free to go, but he had missed his connecting flight to California and had to stay overnight at a hotel close to the airport. Although Tom couldn't get the supervisor to explain exactly what the holdup had been, he was absolutely certain it was due to his previous arrest in Westchester County, where all records and files were to have been sealed and expunged. It was not until six months later and after other incidents of being wrongfully detained when returning from international trips that he finally got an immigration officer to tell him what they were seeing on the computer screen when they checked Tom's passport. According to the officer, a warning message would appear that indicated that there was a criminal investigation in New York pending against Tom.

"Damn that courthouse," Tom thought the instant he learned the news. They were legally obligated to remove all information from the system in addition to being responsible for sealing his records. Clearly, if the U.S. immigration system said he was in the middle of an ongoing criminal investigation, the Westchester County courthouse had failed to honor the commitment that had been made to Tom that all records would be sealed and expunged. Tom shouldn't have been surprised. Apparently, not much had changed in Westchester County since his departure from the crazy woman and the inept Judge.

Chapter 27

In all of the months that Tom had been away from Satha and Westchester County, he had not once given up on his attempt to hold Satha accountable for her promissory note to buy Tom's half of the business from him for $300,000. This amount would not come near to making amends to Tom for all that Satha had taken from him: Tom's money, the 1 Smith Farm Road house that had become a home not only for Tom but also for Ashley and Hercules, most of his personal property within that home, the outdoor camper, his gun collection, his ability to travel freely, his reputation, and more. However, Satha and her attorney were still able to continually delay the case with one specious appeal and motion after another. Her attorney also kept saying that if Tom got a judgment in his favor, Satha was simply going to declare bankruptcy. Although Tom knew that Satha had ill-gotten money stashed in Singapore, he could not prove it and it would be impossible to collect on the judgment. "God, by watching crime stories end on end and with larceny in her heart anyway, she has become one damn smart crook," Tom thought.

Moving on from the nightmare with Satha was only one of the matters that continued to weigh on

Tom's mind. What troubled him far more than anything Satha had ever done to him—as well as his own mistakes in trusting her—was the sad state of the American government, as illustrated by what he had experienced in Westchester County, not to mention what he read and saw in the news every day.

Almost everyone in the country knows that America has the most addled and dysfunctional Congress in modern times – possibly in the nation's history. The executive branch, with the consent of Congress, has the country embroiled in a never ending war against a concept or an action—that of "terror." There is no way to ever declare victory over something as subjective and amorphous as terror. There has always been and, tragically, always will be terror in the world. Of course, Tom thought, we must combat terror whenever it occurs, but to declare it a war makes it "The Perfect War" to the military–industrial complex, as it is a war without an ending. Devaluation of the dollar; massive invasions of privacy conducted by a government spying on its own people, also with the consent of Congress; and invasions of other countries without provocation would all make the Founding Fathers roll in their graves.

And the third branch of American government, the Judiciary, the branch that was established by the Founding Fathers to protect us from government overreach and wrongdoing, is just as messed up as the legislative and executive branches -- maybe more so. Tom reflected on the fact that nothing could illustrate that much better than his own experiences with Westchester County, with Judge Lysander, and with Satha Naar. Yes, the judicial branch, the third leg on the three-legged stool of government set up by the U.S. Constitution, designed to protect citizens against government overreach and tyranny, has also almost completely failed in its duty. If that is true, what's left?

These thoughts and concerns continued to swirl through Tom's head day after day. He found himself pondering them in a particularly poignant way on Independence Day, as he sat on the beach with his daughter Ashley and her friend and watched fireworks burst and sparkle over the Pacific Ocean. Santa Monica had arranged for a philharmonic orchestra to accompany the fireworks, and the way in which the musical performance and the light show were coordinated was magnificent. As the orchestra played the 1812 Overture and patriotic marches of John Philip Sousa, lights of green and gold; lavender and champagne; and, most movingly, red, white, and blue popped in the air and shimmered down the sky in a magical cascade.

The magnificence of the music and the fireworks reminded Tom of what can be created when talented and caring people come together to create something wonderful. Tom reflected on the Founding Fathers and their brilliance in creating a government with a system of checks and balances that, although currently in a state of disrepair, had pretty well stood the test of time.

Can it be brought back and the country once again set on its Constitutional course? Perhaps so, but Tom realized that the country was currently so far off course that it would take a movement of the people—a true groundswell—to get it back on the right track again. Tom loved his country and he believed in the power of the people. As the trumpets sounded, the violins sang, and the fireworks soared, Tom hoped and prayed that American government and democracy would find its way again. But he realized that time is late and action is required NOW!